INDUSTRY / BUSINESS

"No matter how experienced you are, the content and approach in *Buyer-Approved Selling*, will stir your soul! The basic selling process from the buyer's point of view is revealing. This book has some raw truths for everyone in sales... The basics of selling in its purest form!"
—*KEN CARTER, Vice President of Sales, Dana Corporation, Clevite Engine Parts Division*

"All too often the salesperson focuses only on the *sale* without understanding the full depth of the *buyer's* needs. This book brings it back to the basics: building trust and communicating effectively! A good book for every salesperson to read no matter how long they've been selling!"
—*MARK REDMOND, Vice President,*
Worldwide Audio/Video Products, Thomson Multimedia

"This is the book that every sales rep reads and agrees: If they were to write a sales book, this would be it. It's right to the point and validated by buyers... Read it, follow it, and you will grow your business!"
—*BRETT MANLOVE, General Sales Manager, Global Television Network*

"Some of the valuable interactive tools between sales and procurement have been lost in today's fast-paced world. From a buyer's perspective, *Buyer-Approved Selling* brings valuable tools back to the sales professionals."
—*JANE E. MOORE, C.P.M. Senior Buyer, Sara Lee Coffee and Tea*

"Michael Schell's book on sales strategies is a must-read for any sales rep desiring to close the deal with the right person at the right time."
—*TINA M. LOWENTHAL, Associate Director of Purchasing Services,*
California Institute of Technology

"I have just finished the BEST sales book I have ever read. It's called *Buyer-Approved Selling*—and if you sell something I urge you to buy it NOW! Looking at the sales process from the other side of the desk is an invaluable tool—use it!"
—*PAUL SHERMAN, Chairman, Ecademy Marketplace UK*

"I am responsible for a direct sales force that calls on the very buyers you analyze in *Buyer-Approved Selling*. We are always looking for a better way to communicate our message with these buyers. Your book tells us exactly what selling strategies they appreciate most. How valuable is that!"
—*GARY HUBBARD, Senior Vice-President, Liberty Northwest Insurance*

"Sales professionals spend their entire careers learning to put themselves in the customer's shoes. This book will help rookies and veterans alike by giving them the perspective they need—the customer's perspective!"
—*BRAD BALLANCE, VP of Sales, Toshiba Information Systems Group*

"*Buyer-Approved Selling* is a very practical book for anyone involved in business development. A good example is the GPOS (Genuine Preemptive Objection Statement—the key word here is 'genuine'). I agree… The sales professional should preempt objections by demonstrating value upfront in the appropriate areas, and should focus on achieving a balanced exchange of common interests between both parties. This book is a must-read (and—practice) for every sales professional that cares."
—*GERARD DARMON, CEO, Dexior Financial Inc.*

"Our salespeople sell to the engineering community… Integrating the supply chain and procurement function into the account-planning process is critical. Communicating effectively at this level and understanding the complexities of the customers' requirements in a global marketplace are necessary for long-term success, and as such, *Buyer-Approved Selling* is a must-read for our team."
—*RAYMOND J. CANZANESE, V.P. Sales and Marketing, Southco Inc.*

"Successful account executives know, understand, and use this approach to selling. Why wouldn't you? It's what the buyer is looking for. The material in this book—the buyer's insights and perspectives—is what every sales professional should understand. It's required reading in my territory because my staff, our organization, and ultimately our customers will benefit."
—*RICK BURKHALTER, Regional Vice President, Liberty Northwest Insurance*

"My professional football career in the NFL taught me a lot of ways to develop the winning edge. Number one: Always have a solid strategy and game plan. Number two: Know and study what the other guy is thinking. *Buyer-Approved Selling* is the winning-edge strategy to compete in today's world of professional sales."
—*MARK WALCZAK, former NFL & CFL Football player and real estate and investment sales professional*

"… Michael Schell surveyed buyers about what salespeople do wrong and in *Buyer-Approved Selling*… sets out a process to meet buyers' needs, from prospecting to post-sales communication. The book presents some innovative ideas and offers useful questions to integrate into your sales routine, but even better is hearing the voices of buyers throughout commenting on the techniques and pointing to the preferred path. The book would benefit most salespeople."

—HARVEY SCHACHTER, The Globe and Mail

"Schell's book is refreshingly direct and wastes little time preaching or pontificating about the bad habits of salespeople. He lets the customers he's interviewed do that for him… and it works. Consider *Buyer-Approved Selling* a 'scared-straight' program for sales reps. After reading it, your sales team may well declare, 'We have met the enemy, and he is us'."

—NATHAN MALLETT, Editor, Sales Promotion Magazine

"Many books focus on the 'how' without explaining the 'why.' *Buyer-Approved Selling* blends the best of both worlds—concrete suggestions [with] real-world explanations."

—LAIN EHMANN, Freelance Business Journalist

"I've seen my share of books on salesmanship and they're all about selling technique. Mike Schell's book addresses the disconnect all salespeople suffer from: viewing the selling process from the buyer's perspective. If all salespeople could read Mike's book, it would save us prospects a lot of time and energy."

—BRAD FORSYTHE, Creator & Co-Host, The Advertising Show

"You can't communicate, connect, or sell successfully without feedback. *Buyer-Approved Selling* is a feedback treasure-trove."

—NICHOLAS BOOTHMAN, author of How to Connect in Business in 90 Seconds or Less

"Getting it right from the buyer's point of view—in today's marketplace, there is no Plan B. Read this book—it's important and it will help you make a difference in regard to something that matters!"

—*RICHARD RUFF, President of Sales Momentum and co-author of* Managing Major Sales *and* Getting Partnering Right

"Too many salespeople have the misfortune of working for sales managers who were promoted because of their sales ability, not their management talent. This book is a self-help guide for such salespeople."

—*MIKE BOSWORTH, Author of* Solution Selling *and co-author of* CustomerCentric Selling

EDUCATION

"In today's business world, sales reps must understand the buyer's perspective to succeed. This book will open your eyes to that reality."

—*DANE CHRISTENSEN, NW Region, Director of Marketing, University of Phoenix*

"Overall, this book is a good read and a high-quality educational tool for sales practitioners, corporate sales trainers, and academic educators. The application content and wealth of buyer insights provided in this book clearly differentiate it from contemporary sales textbooks. Also, its research foundation differentiates it from many of the other trade books targeted at sales professionals. Regardless of the reader's level of sales experience, they will discover that Schell delivers on the promise of his book's title. Refreshing!"

—*E. STEPHEN GRANT MBA PhD, University of New Brunswick*
Journal of the Academy of Marketing Science, *Volume 32 Issue 01 pp 99-100*
©*2004 by Sage Publications, Inc. Reprinted by Permission of Sage Publications, Inc.*

"I enjoyed reading Michael Schell's book *Buyer-Approved Selling*. Michael and his team did a great job [with] their research and the analysis of the data. This book is an asset for both students and existing salespeople as it clearly demonstrates the tactical 'how-to's' of successful selling. Michael's research underscores the need to plan, listen, follow-up and continuously improve your personal development as a salesperson."

—*DAVID MOULTON, Marketing Instructor,*
School of Business, Kwantlen University College

Sales Secrets
from the
Buyer's Side
of the
Desk

Read Today...Use Tomorrow

THE
APPROVED
SERIES

™

BUYER
APPROVED

PUBLICATIONS™

SELLING

Foreword by
Christopher Locke,
Global Lead Buyer,
DaimlerChrysler Corporation

MICHAEL SCHELL

Buyer-Approved Selling:
Sales Secrets from the Buyer's Side of the Desk

Senior editors: Andy Fielding, Mitch Merker, Paul Goudie
Associate editors: Michelle Seidel, Eva Nerelius, Arlene Prunkl, Patricia Anderson, PhD

Published by Approved Publications Inc.
Suite 208 - 700 West Pender Street
Vancouver, British Columbia
V6C 1G8

Call us toll-free: 1-877-870-0009

Visit our website: www.approvedseries.com

National Library of Canada Cataloguing in Publication Data

Schell, Michael, 1959-
Buyer-Approved Selling: sales secrets from the buyer's side of the desk / Michael Schell.

Includes bibliographical references and index.
ISBN 0-9731675-0-5

1. Selling. 2. Sales management. I. Title.
HF5438.25.S33 2003   658.85   C2003-910004-9

Cover design: Rocks DeHart Public Relations
Formatting: Fortunato Aglialoro

Printed in Canada

In memory of my cousin
Andrew Douglas Schell
1969 – 2001

TABLE OF CONTENTS

SECTION 1: PROSPECTING

SECTION 2: PREPARING

SECTION 3: MEETING

SECTION 4: PROPOSING

SECTION 5: CLOSING

SECTION 6: MAINTAINING

SECTION 7: COMMUNICATING

SECTION 8: ANNOYING

GRATITUDE

It's great to have a dream, but it takes good people to help you make a dream come true. This book is a reality because of the work of an incredible, inspiring team of friends and colleagues.

My good friend and fellow Director of Approved Publications and Training, Jason Foyle, was directly responsible for setting up our book research facilities in Vancouver. My valued friend Mitch Merker, CEO of the Marketshare Research Institute and senior editor of this book, provided incredible support, enthusiasm, mind-power, time, humor and resilience. My good friend Eva Nerelius, Business Operations Manager of Approved Publications and Training, edited content and spent many late-nights poring over charts and data. Paul Goudie gave his passion, skill and unwavering support.

My research team was relentless in their pursuit of the information this project required. Research Coordinator Tanya Rauser spearheaded their efforts, spending countless hours contacting participants and organizing their responses. Researchers Clarice Abadilla, Vijay Anand, Jessica Andrews, Teresa Bailey, Mark Bourgeois, Åsa Nerelius, Joanna Bryniarska, Andrew Carson, Sean Cunningham, Shezmeen Hudani, Bianca Knop, Duncan Lea, Serena Lin, Jenna Lopez, Gordon Nesbitt, Don Roberts, Terri Rowson, Cassandra Stephens and Frances Ubalde did an amazing job of cold-calling, interviewing and collecting feedback from some of the busiest, hardest-to-reach decision-makers in North America.

My dedicated editorial team demanded excellence. Arlene Prunkl, Michelle Seidel and Patricia Anderson, PhD, conducted the initial round of edits, followed by Mitch Merker, Paul Goudie, Eva Nerelius and Andy Fielding. They always arrived early and stayed late to make this book happen. In particular, I appreciate Andy's simplification ideas; they helped us create concise material that sales professionals could use "right out of the box".

Rocks DeHart Public Relations did an amazing job designing the cover and took the time to get the look just right. Andy Fielding designed the charts and Fortunato Aglialoro carefully formatted the content.

My uncle Joseph Schell took on the considerable task of compiling the chart data. Mark Savard and Mitch Owens made some valuable last-minute editing suggestions.

Christopher Locke of DaimlerChrysler, Greg Tennyson of Oracle Corporation, Mitch Bardwell of Canon U.S.A., and Troy Blanchette of Avnet Applied Computing Solutions generously allowed their endorsements to appear on the cover, and Christopher provided an excellent foreword as well. Dr. Harry Hough, President of the American Purchasing Society, kindly promoted our project in his *Professional Purchasing Newsletter*.

Nicholas Boothman, Richard Ruff, Mike Bosworth, Ken Carter, Nathan Mallett, Lain Ehmann, Brad Forsythe, Harvey Schachter, Mark Redmond, Brett Manlove, Jane E. Moore, Tina Lowenthal, Paul Sherman, Gary Hubbard, Brad Ballance, David Moulton, Raymond J. Canzanese, Rick Burkhalter, Mark Walczak and Dane Christensen generously allowed their endorsements to appear at the beginning pages of this book.

Three insightful authors kindly allowed me to include excerpts from their books: Jill Konrath, Art Sobczak, and Bob Kantin.

Dr. Stephen Grant, PhD, and countless other friends and associates, reviewed this material at every stage of its development and gave it the benefit of their objective opinions and criticisms.

Bill and Joyce Foyle provided much support, and an incredible atmosphere for writing, at their Raven's Pass.

The Panel of Professional Purchasers shared their knowledge, experience, and unique perspectives.

I want to thank the incredibly talented team at Dexior Financial Inc., especially Gerard Darmon, Sai Jiwani Mohamed, Sanja Spasojevic and Marc Poitras for their unflagging support and sage advice, which have proven invaluable.

Finally, my mother Angela Hannaford and nephew Ben Schell motivated me to stay focused on this project and see it through.

To all of you, my sincere thanks!

HALF PRICE BOOKS ®

Half Price Books
3860 LA REUNION PKWY
DALLAS, TX 75212
OFS OrderID   15461519

‖‖‖‖‖‖‖‖‖‖‖‖

SKU	ISBN/UPC	Title & Author/Artist	Shelf ID	Qty	OrderSKU
S285285806	9780973167511	Buyer-Approved Selling: Sales Secrets from.... Michael Schell	BUS 4.6	1	‖‖‖‖‖‖‖

Visit our stores to sell your books, music, movies games for cash.

SHIPPED STANDARD TO:
Tina Huber
310 Pleasant view ct
Copiague NY 11726

ORDER# **113-9728387-5321838**
AmazonMarketplaceUS

Thank you for your order, Tina Huber!

Thank you for shopping with Half Price Books! Please contact service109@hpb.com. if you have any questions, comments or concerns about your order (113-9728387-5321838)

I am a *buyer.* In a typical day, I have numerous meetings with suppliers who hand me brochures and give presentations designed to show me what their companies can do for me. Rarely does a supplier ask me what I actually want.

I also have sales meetings with suppliers who can't understand why they rarely, if ever, get an order from me. They spend their time and energy criticizing the purchasing process, instead of focusing their time and energy on correcting previous mistakes and improving their prospects with me.

In both cases, I sit in my chair and gaze across the table at them, and think, "If I were a supplier, I know what I would do to satisfy my customer and increase future business."

That's what this book is all about: the *buyer's* point of view. It's about the lessons learned over years of requests-for-quotes, supplier lineup meetings, quote evaluations, negotiating, and purchase-order placement.

This book is an insight into the psyche of a buyer. It's an x-ray of the buyer's brain—of what the buyer is really thinking, but for political reasons may not articulate. It covers the buyer's goals, desires, and frustrations—from the smallest of supplier oversights to the largest of commercial blunders. It's the buyer's inner voice bellowing out, "Hey you, what part of this commercial obligation didn't you understand?"

This book gives professional sales reps a look into the world of the people who purchase from them. It gives them a chance to walk around in the buyer's shoes. It offers them a competitive edge and an opportunity for future growth.

This book gives the supplier the means to improve commerce, to improve profits, and most importantly, to improve relationships. My only wish is that suppliers read this book with a thirst to improve the way they do business, and thus reduce their vulnerability in the ever-changing market.

CHRISTOPHER LOCKE
Global Lead Buyer
DaimlerChrysler Corporation

INTRODUCTION

A few years ago, after twenty years in corporate sales, I decided to start my own company. Now it was my turn in the buyer's seat. With the tables turned and sales reps pitching to me, I realized how rarely reps asked insightful questions. Many of them were from leading companies, yet they disregarded basics like setting agendas for meetings and doing research before the call. It showed a lack of respect for my time, and made me question their reliability and accountability. It also made me take my business elsewhere. Life is too short, and business too important, to allow others to waste my time.

This shift in perspective, from sales professional to business owner, was like being hit on the head with a hammer. I realized clearly that the single biggest contributor to success in sales is to switch your focus from working *in* your job to working *on* your job. That is the difference that makes the difference.

Switching to the buyer's side of the desk has given me a greater appreciation of a sales rep's responsibilities. These include

- Exploring and identifying needs
- Remembering details
- Honoring promises
- Confirming commitments

- Avoiding assumptions about a prospect's business

- Communicating with clarity

As a buyer, I like to deal with people who communicate concisely, knowledgeably, proactively, and dependably. I don't like to deal with people who waste my time, who make promises they don't keep, and who come to me only 60 percent prepared. I want 100 percent effort and ability from the people I *choose* to deal with.

As it relates to sales, the 80/20 principle means that 20 percent of sales professionals close 80 percent of the business. The other 80 percent of the reps fall into the "average" category and don't see the same results for their efforts. This means there is tremendous opportunity for the sales professional who wants to be a standout, a member of the elite class.

I saw the need for a book written from the perspective of experienced buyers who had met and interacted with countless sales reps over the years. Who better to help a sales professional to sell than a professional buyer?

For the purpose of this book, we can consider the decision-maker to be a prospect, a buyer, a purchaser, a procurement specialist, and so on. Consider that buyers may not always have the authority to say "yes" to a purchase decision, but they almost always have the power to say "no."

This book is a practical guide and workbook for sales professionals and their managers. Effective selling requires you to differentiate yourself from the competition. Some of the tips and strategies in this book require extra planning and preparation, but when you're selling to your major accounts, you simply cannot afford to waste your opportunities. You must be at the top of your game. Remember, your competition wants the business too, and they are undoubtedly sending in their best people to close the deal.

So here it is at your fingertips: Feedback from experienced, professional buyers. These corporate decision-makers have shared their opinions and advice on how to do your job better—to win more of their business. Read the book, do the planning guides, and enjoy the success that comes from going the extra mile.

ABOUT THIS BOOK

A note from Mitch Merker, CEO of the Marketshare Research Institute. One of the key elements that add value to this book is the quality and integrity of the research. As such, I've outlined some statistics to illustrate our approach to the buyer interviews.

The Process We made thousands of phone calls and interviewed hundreds of corporate sales trainers, sales reps, and sales managers from companies across the U.S. to gather the most effective sales strategies used in corporate America today.

We then presented these strategies to purchasing professionals from over 200 companies across America for their ratings and comments.

- Total number of buyers: **228**
- Total number of interviews: **330**
- Total number of questions: **4,327**

The Buyers We were fortunate to have such a tremendous Buyers Panel. Our buyers had an average of over 17 years' experience, and many carried certifications including

- Certified Purchasing Professional (CPP)
- Certified Professional Purchasing Manager (CPPM)
- Certified Purchasing Manager (C.P.M.)
- Accredited Purchasing Practitioner (A.P.P.)

Most of the buyers we approached received our book concept with enthusiasm. Even when buyers had to decline our invitation due to time constraints, they usually said, "It's about time somebody asked *our* opinions on the sales process." All of the buyers who contributed to this book were helpful and candid.

The Companies We surveyed a variety of companies: Smaller firms with 50 to 100 employees; major corporations such as DaimlerChrysler, Oracle Corporation, Sara Lee and Verizon, with hundreds of thousands of employees; and companies in between. Industries included:

- Manufacturing

- Telecommunications

- Education

- Financial Services

- Aerospace

- Software

- Printing

- Health

- Hospitality

- Entertainment

Use of Panel Member and Company Names Where a buyer's or their company's name appears with comments, it's because we received their permission to use it. Where a comment is labeled *Anonymous*, or no company name appears, consent was not available.

Mitch Merker, CEO
Marketshare Research Institute

WHY THIS BOOK WILL WORK FOR YOU

When we asked professional buyers to define the essence of effective selling, they consistently cited three key areas:

- Effective communication
- Building trust
- Respecting time

Imagine one of your clients is talking about you. This client is saying that you never waste their time, that you communicate with them on a high level, and that they can trust you completely. What kind of behavior receives that kind of praise?

This book tells you, in a step-by-step format. The buyers have rated and approved each sales approach, and personally commented on many of them. When you see that buyers value a certain approach you are not using, and you read why they value it, you have a catalyst for action.

The book offers you another catalyst: the charts of the buyers' overall responses. They graphically show that most reps *do not use* many of the Buyer-Approved approaches. The message is clear: Here are excellent ways to differentiate yourself from other reps!

Selling the Buyer-Approved way is not about gimmicks or new, "undiscovered" sales tactics. It is about establishing trust, communicating clearly, and making the most of your buyers' time—and specific ways to do it.

It's said that "time is the currency of business." That's why, throughout this book, you'll see a special emphasis on time. It can be distilled to this basic statement:

Don't waste the buyer's time!

Our buyers said it again and again: When you plan and prepare for initial contacts, for meetings, and for follow-ups, you respect and save the buyer's time—and you really stand out. You become a valued resource. This cannot be overemphasized.

To help you prepare to make the most of your prospects' time, this book shows you how to

✔ Research your prospects

✔ Prepare concise statements about your business

✔ Prepare questions

✔ Anticipate common objections

✔ Prepare for tough questions

✔ Prepare an advance agenda, and invite changes to it

✔ Prepare objective questions for buyers to consider with any supplier

and other essential pre-contact steps. It goes on to show you how to maximize your prospects' time when you meet with them, and in your subsequent contacts.

Buyer-Approved Selling covers every stage of the sales process, and gives you the details you need to use specific approaches that work.

If you consistently follow these methods, you will have your best chance at becoming one of the top 20% of sales professionals—those who are considered such valued resources that their clients consistently refer them to new prospects. *Imagine never having to cold call again!* That potential is yours when you start selling the Buyer-Approved way.

PROSPECTING

Prospecting, cold-calling, business development, dialing for dollars—no matter what you call it, for most sales pros, it's a necessary part of the job. You may consider it your least-enjoyable task, until it brings you an appointment with a big company. Then it gets exciting.

The goal of this section is to help you overcome the challenges of new business development by giving you useful, practical approaches that will help you make calls with confidence and set qualified appointments.

What's more, these approaches are Buyer-Approved—so once you've customized them to your needs, you can use them with confidence.

I'll leave you now to enjoy the read, and to develop your own ISPS and KPS. See you again in Section 2.

—Mike

 **Secret 1** **Database Management**

How effective would you be if you approached your territory without a game plan? Maximizing results from your prospecting efforts requires proper planning and preparation.

You may already have a strategy for managing and prioritizing your territory's prospect database—but if you don't, you will benefit by implementing this systematic approach to effective prospecting:

1. Compile or create your total prospect list.

2. Prioritize and number your list according to each prospect's potential.

3. From this master list, create a new list for each industry type. Since you have numbered your original list in the order of each prospect's potential, your new vertical market lists will also be in that order. (Note: You can refer to these lists when creating your ISPS in Secret 2.)

"I get irritated when a rep truly does not understand the products they are selling and the applications of that product. This happens far too often for our liking. The problem seems to be that companies hire good salespeople but not good industry-specific people."

— *JIM MOREY, Vice President of Procurement, Sara Lee Foods, a division of Sara Lee Corporation*

 **Secret 2** | **The Industry-Specific Positioning Statement (ISPS)**

The buyer's side of the desk: Imagine you're a buyer who receives an average of four cold calls a day. That's almost 1,000 cold calls each year! How annoyed would you be when sales reps called to tell you all the great things their company could do for you—when it was clear they were not tuned in to your specific needs?

Now consider how refreshing it would be to hear from a rep who was a *specialist* in your field.

Be a specialist! Develop an Industry-Specific Positioning Statement (ISPS) for each vertical market you target. Learn and become conversant in the vernacular of the industry. It's natural that people prefer to deal with experts who understand their specific industry's needs and challenges.

When you introduce your company on a first phone call or in a first meeting, your ISPS can help stimulate your prospect's interest and curiosity. It introduces you as an industry specialist, and tells the prospect that you can increase revenues or reduce costs. It is a sentence that crystallizes the main benefits of doing business with your company.

Think of the business people you know. How many of them can express the essence of their company's business in a single well-constructed sentence? It's easy—and often fun—to find out: Ask some of your business colleagues to describe what their company does, and the key benefits to their customers, in 15 words or fewer.

ISPS Examples: If you are selling inventory management software to the electronic manufacturing industry, you might say:

"We specialize in lowering inventory management costs for electronics manufacturers."

Similarly, your targets may be universities and colleges, whose primary objective is to increase revenue through higher enrollment. In this case, your ISPS could be:

"We're enrollment-creation specialists for the educational industry."

If you were selling corporate long distance services, your ideal client is someone whose calls are primarily under a minute in length. Since your company offers billing in six-second increments, you can provide them with significant savings. A great ISPS to use for the call center industry could be:

"We specialize in reducing minimum billing costs for the call center industry."

Planning Guide:

Creating an ISPS

Step 1: Using the lists you made in Step 3 of Secret 1, create a list of specific companies you want to target.

Step 2: Identify and learn the industry vernacular while researching each company's website. Write down key words and phrases for potential use in your ISPS.

Step 3: Find out which associations serve the industry, and write their names here. Research their websites and publications to understand the current state of that vertical market.

Step 4: Identify the key benefits your product or service offers this market.

Step 5: Write the ISPS.

- Try to limit your ISPS to 15 words. Remember, your objective is to *quickly* determine a potential fit with your prospect.

- Emphasize how you can increase revenues or decrease expenses.

- Become so familiar with your ISPS that it is second nature to you.

The Buyers Comment

**Wm. Frank Quiett,
C.P.M., A.P.P.,**
*Project Lead,
Supply Chain Management
and Strategic Sourcing*

"Excellent approach. The key here is to increase your knowledge, not to learn new buzzwords to sell with, but a real, honest-to-goodness knowledge base you can apply to the customer's industry-specific needs. Surface knowledge will get you in the door, but having a real working knowledge of the processes, requirements, and solutions will keep you there!"

Erik Schlichting,
Inventory Control Manager

"There is nothing more irritating than someone who doesn't understand the pressures specific to my industry … This approach is an excellent way for a sales rep to learn about our business and be prepared."

Judy Elrite, C.P.M.,
Buyer Specialist

"I get calls all the time and the salespeople seem to either patronize or fumble. If they knew what my company did, and knew more about our industry, they would be smoother and much less annoying. I don't think I should have to teach them how to sell to my industry."

Peter Van der Hoek,
Buyer/Planner

"If a rep could identify my industry type, our position in the market, and my company's needs, I would be impressed. I would feel more comfortable working with someone who has taken the time to learn about our industry."

Christopher Locke,
*Global Lead Buyer,
DaimlerChrysler Corporation*

"About 50 percent of my suppliers use this approach. The other 50 percent tend to focus on their company history and prior accomplishments rather than the benefits and opportunities for the client. They talk about *their* company instead of *mine*."

The buyers comment *cont'd*

Charles Tobler,
C.P.M, M.P.P.,
Senior Buyer

"If this were done correctly, it would be a buyer's dream. It would be a great asset to understand our industry, and it would make it easier to explore mutual possibilities."

Grahame Gill,
Facilities Buyer

"If a sales rep called me and used this approach effectively, there's a good chance he would get an appointment to meet with me."

 **Secret 3** | **The Primary Reason Statement (PRS)**

In situations where an ISPS isn't appropriate, consider using a *Primary Reason Statement* (PRS).

For example, if your company has never sold anything to a particular industry, an ISPS wouldn't work. You couldn't validly claim experience in that particular field.

The PRS is a single sentence that identifies your line of business and tells your prospect the primary reason that companies do business with you. Simply structure your PRS by combining your line of business with the word "specialists" or "specialize" to highlight your company's ability to increase revenues or decrease expenses in a specific area.

Examples:

- "We're a corporate long-distance provider, and we specialize in reducing minimum billing costs."

- "We're a software company and we specialize in lowering inventory-management costs."

 **Secret 4** | **Key Point Statements (KPS)**

> ***The buyer's side of the desk:*** Buyers tell us they hear a lot of long-winded reasons why they should set an appointment with a cold-calling rep. Clearly these reps have not taken the time to create and rehearse clearly articulated statements of the key reasons why companies do business with them.

Key Point Statements deliver clear, concise information about your company/product/service—especially when you have limited time to get your point across and need to make a quick impact.

Two well-written Key Point Statements that can be conveyed in 15 seconds or less can be very effective—not only for cold calls, but in chance encounters with prospects ("elevator speeches"). Remember: Key Point Statements are not sales presentations, so keep them brief. (We will incorporate your Key Point Statements in the *permission-based cold call guide* in Secret 6.)

Example: *A company that sells long-distance services to businesses.*

Step 1: List the four key points you want to make during the call:

- Your customers include Fortune 500 companies.

- Your time is billed in four-second increments.

- You have the lowest per-minute rate in the country.

- You're a stable, publicly-owned company.

Step 2: Use *any two key points* from your list above to create your two Key Point Statements.

■ We've been around for 15 years, and we're a stable, publicly-owned company with a number of Fortune 500 clients.

■ At three cents a minute, our corporate long-distance rates are the lowest in the country—and we bill in four-second increments.

Planning Guide:

Identify the four key points you will use in your Key Point Statements. Use the two that best go together to create the first half of your Key Point Statement. Then combine the remaining two to conclude your statement.

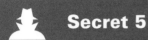 **Secret 5** | **Basic Pre-Call Research**

Buyer's side of the desk: Imagine you're a buyer who receives 1,000 cold calls a year. Would you be likely to give appointments to sales reps who asked questions that showed a complete unfamiliarity with your business? That's why it's important to do some basic research on your prospect companies before you call them.

If you sort your prospects by industry type (Secret 1) and create your ISPS (Secret 2), you should be ready to make intelligent initial calls to most of the people on your list. However, for your *key* prospects (where you may face more competition), you should prepare even further by doing some more extensive research on those companies.

You may not always have time to research your key prospects as deeply as you'd like. At minimum, try to find answers to these questions:

1. How many locations do they have, and is this the head office?

2. Has the company been in the news or had other publicity in the last six months?

3. Who are their major customers?

4. What are their main product/service lines?

5. What are their major industry challenges?

"I prefer to be asked for a moment of my time, but only about 20% of sales reps ever do that."

— *LORI PATTEN, Director of Projects—Development, Hyatt Hotels Corporation*

"Most of the reps who call on me don't ask permission for my time. When they do ask, and I don't have time, I usually show my appreciation by trying to schedule a future call."

— *TINA M. LOWENTHAL, Associate Director, Purchasing Services, California Institute of Technology*

 **Secret 6** **The Permission-Based Cold Call**

Buyer's side of the desk: Imagine you're a buyer who receives cold calls every day. It's your job to take these calls—but it's also your job to select the most appropriate people to meet. How would you feel about sales reps who launched directly into their pitches the moment you picked up the phone, showing no regard for your time?

Your first call to your prospect has one goal: setting a qualified appointment. If you've completed the steps in Secrets 1 through 4, it's simple to customize your own calling guide using the Buyer-Approved *permission-based cold call model*.

Some conventional sales trainers think you should open cold calls by immediately delivering a key benefit, without first asking for a moment of the prospect's time. They believe that asking permission gives the prospect a chance to shut down the call before it begins.

However, could this lack of courtesy start you off on the wrong foot, and make you seem invasive and annoying? The answer seems to be *yes*.

Marketshare has used a permission-based approach in over 150,000 cold calls. These calls were made to prospects in 33 cities across America, in a variety of industries, including

- Accounting

- Software

- Higher Education

- Business Associations

- Professional Sports

- Financial Services

- Office Equipment

- Corporate Training

An impressive *eighty-five percent* of the prospects responded favorably and agreed to proceed with the call. Of the remaining fifteen percent, the vast majority simply asked to be called again at a more convenient time. Using permission-based call models, Marketshare has set over 8000 appointments with busy decision-makers across America. These statistics indicate that you should feel confident using this model, regardless of your business type or location.

The Permission-Based Cold Call Model

Use the model below to create your own permission-based guide for seeking appointments. This model assumes you have identified the decision-maker for your products or services.

(1) Ask for permission to open the call

"Hi, Monica, this is Cassandra from ABC Co. I don't need much time—do you have a 'quick minute'?"

(2) Present your ISPS or PRS

"Thanks, Monica. We specialize in reducing minimum billing costs for the call-center industry."

(3) Determine the prospect's level of knowledge of your company, product or service

"Are you familiar with/have you ever used/do you know much about [choose one]:

- Our company?
- This process?
- This type of service?
- This product?
- This kind of application?"

(4) Ask for permission to present your Key Point Statements

"Is it okay if I tell you a couple of key points about us/ what we do / our product / this process?"

(5) Present your Key Point Statements

"We're a stable, publicly-owned company with a number of Fortune 500 clients, and we've been in business for 15 years."

"We bill long-distance calls in four-second increments, and at three cents a minute, our corporate long-distance rates are the lowest in the country."

(6) Ask your qualifying question

"Monica, I have a quick question for you. Based on what I've told you so far, can you see any potential for ABC Co. to be of value to your business, either now or at some point down the road?"

(7) Ask for the appointment

"Monica, it would be great if I could stop by to see if we can help you out in any way. Are you available next Thursday? I won't waste your time."

Prospect: Yes, I'll be here.

"Great, would 10:30 work for you?"

Prospect: No, I'm in meetings until noon.

"Ok, how about 3 p.m.?"

(8) Confirm the appointment

"Perfect. Just to confirm, then: I'll meet you at your office, 1070 Main Street, at 3 p.m. on Thursday, June the first. Did I get that right?"

"Monica, can I leave my contact details with you?
(Leave your name and number)
Thanks Monica, I'll see you next Thursday."

(9) Supplements to the permission-based cold call model

When they don't have a "quick minute"

When you ask, "Do you have a 'quick minute'?", your prospect may say, "No, it's not a good time." Marketshare's experience suggests that this response is most effective:

"Is it okay if I give you a call back some other time?"

Answer: "Yes, that's fine."

"Thanks, when would be the best time for me to call you back?"

When they just want information

One common response during a cold call is, "Can you just send me some information?" To effectively handle this question, consider these responses:

"Monica, I could send information, but in the interest of saving your time, how's this?: I've developed a ten-minute meeting (*see Secret 8*) designed to identify our potential value to you—ten minutes and I'm out the door. I won't waste your time."

If prospect declines:

"Shall I email you a link to our website, or do you prefer printed information in the mail?"

(Prospect replies)

"Ok, I'll get that out to you today. Can I give you a quick call next Friday to see if a meeting makes sense for you then?"

"Using voicemail to leave a message or sales pitch is meaningless without personal interaction. People are tired of machine-to-machine voice tag; make the effort to contact them personally."

— *WM. FRANK QUIETT, C.P.M., A.P.P., Project Lead,*
Supply Chain Management and Strategic Sourcing

 **Secret 7** ## No Voicemail Cold Calls

Buyer's side of the desk: Imagine you're a buyer. How likely is it that you'll have the time to return a continual barrage of unsolicited voicemail from sales reps you don't know, selling things you may not even need? Is that an effective way to initiate contact with a prospect? We asked the buyers: Should a rep you've never spoken to leave voicemail to make first contact?

The overwhelming response was: Don't clog the buyer's voicemail with unsolicited messages when making cold calls.

The Buyers Comment

Don Walraven, *Director of Inventory Management,* *Alaska Distributors Co.*	"No, I don't like voicemail for initial contact. Sales reps should try again until they get through."
Greg Adkins, *Purchasing Manager*	"It's better for a salesperson to keep calling until they get hold of me. It is in their best interest to do so, since in most cases, I'm busy and may have to delete the message and move on."
Paula L. Martin, *Corporate IT Buyer*	"No, I very seldom return voicemail from reps who are prospecting. If I did that, I would be calling forty people a day. Is there a better way? Call until I answer the phone."
Crystal Leonard, *Buyer-Indirect*	"I want reps to keep trying until they get me. Voicemail does not work with buyers. I have too much to do and cannot call people back when I have never talked to them before."
Carl Colasurdo, *Director of Purchasing*	"I don't suggest a rep leave voicemail for initial contact. Keep calling until I answer."

"A 10-minute meeting is a very ambitious objective. That promise may get you in the door — ONCE. To ensure you are on the road to building a partnership, you must accomplish what you have promised. You should work to stay on track, keep focused on the points you wish to make, and close your presentation with opportunities for cost-reduction. In today's economy, more and more buyers are operating under a cost-reduction charter from upper management. If you can help them achieve this goal, they will be more likely to listen and be open to further discussions."

— *LYNNE E. GEHRKE, Vice President, Procurement, A. B. Dick Company*

 **Secret 8** ## The Ten-Minute Meeting

Buyer's side of the desk: When you're a buyer with limited time, choosing the sales reps you deal with is a matter of risk/reward. Reps who waste buyers' time with unprepared, unstructured meetings fall in the high-risk category, no matter how charming and likable they may be. Times have changed, and most of the buyers we spoke to agreed: The days of socializing sales calls are over.

Sales reps are constantly calling buyers to set first-time appointments. If a buyer meets with only two new reps a week, that adds up to a hundred new reps in a year. Most reps are taught that people buy only from reps they like and trust, so it's no wonder that they try to spend the first ten minutes of their initial meetings on so-called "relationship-building" small talk.

But what do buyers think about this? Do they want small talk? According to our research, the answer is no.

Our research shows that buyers prefer reps who respect their limited time by stating, up-front, that they have prepared a structured meeting, with the objective of determining if there is a fit that supports further discussion at the buyer's convenience.

Consider this approach:

"Monica, I know you're busy. I've prepared a ten-minute meeting agenda that will quickly determine if our company can be of value to you. When could we meet for ten minutes? I guarantee I won't waste your time."

To prepare for an effective ten-minute meeting

- Research the prospect's company.
- Define your meeting objective.
- Prepare and rehearse a brief overview of your company.
- Prepare intelligent, insightful questions.
- Rehearse your ten-minute power meeting with a colleague.

It's amazing what you can accomplish in ten minutes when you stay focused. Let's assume you employ the ten-minute meeting, and it leads to an ongoing business relationship. Continuing to set brief, structured meetings is a good way to maintain the relationship. You avoid being perceived as a risk to the buyer's limited time. The buyer is more likely to retain your company as a supplier, and to give you referrals.

Note: In Secret 16 we introduce the Advance Meeting Agenda (AMA). In the case of the initial ten-minute meeting, you've already stated the objective so an AMA is not required. Your time is limited; you'll need every available second to go through your company overview and ask the questions you prepared.

The Buyers Comment

Yvonne Ventimiglia,
Division Manager,
Leverage Purchasing,
Layne Christensen Company

"This approach shows respect for my time. Also, when a busy buyer is swamped with back-to-back meetings, this allows five or ten minutes in between to check phone messages etc. It is not pleasant to be escorting someone out of the office while another one waits."

Paula L. Martin,
Corporate IT Buyer

"Time is valuable, so I think it's a great idea!"

Anonymous

"Most first meetings are too long. This approach sounds like it could be a time-saver."

Wendy Imamura,
C.P.M., CPPB, CMIR,
Material Processing Center
Manager, Verizon Hawaii Inc.

"Yes, I believe a power meeting can be a good door-opener."

"If the interest was there, I would attend. All things being equal, this has the potential to influence my decision to a large degree. Properly executed, this type of activity could save a lot of wasted time."

— *RICHARD K. TYLER, C.P.M., Director of Purchasing, MRC Bearings*

 **Secret 9** **Objective Information-Based Seminars**

Position your company as experts in their industry by conducting practical, informative seminars. This can generate positive awareness among the companies you target, and give your existing clients additional value.

The subject matter doesn't have to be entirely related to your product or service, but it must be of value to your target audience.

Ideas for an Effective Seminar

- Keep your seminar between 45 and 90 minutes.

- Provide *objective*, useful information. The seminar should not be a sales pitch.

- Set up a table at the back of the room with additional information such as brochures or content from the seminar. Make it available, but not mandatory.

- Following the presentation, give the participants a chance to interact. For some attendees, networking can be the most valuable part of the session.

- Provide a feedback form for attendees. Include sections for comments and ideas for future events.

- Mail each participant a letter thanking them for attending. If they provided feedback, consider referring to it in the letter.

Examples:

- A security company hosts a seminar on workplace violence.

- A software company hosts a seminar on computer security.

We asked the Buyers: What percentage of reps offer informational seminars?

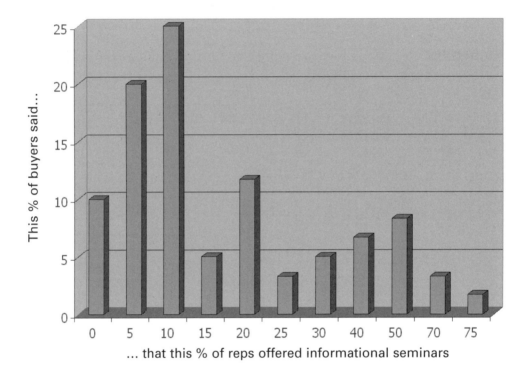

Summary: The majority of the buyers said that the number of reps offering informational seminars **only amounted to 15% or less**.

We asked the Buyers: On a scale of 1 to 10 (10 being highest), to what degree do informational seminars influence your decision to buy?

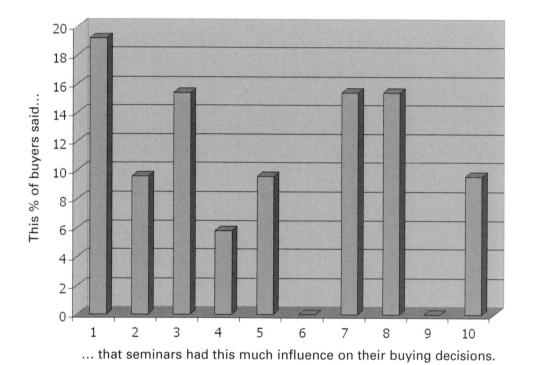

... that seminars had this much influence on their buying decisions.

Summary: Almost half of the buyers said that effective informational seminars **positively influenced** their buying decisions.

The Buyers Comment

Kenneth F. Esbin,
Purchasing Manager,
Tarmac America

"We're currently in the process of negotiating a very large contract with a number of potential suppliers. The deciding factors will be the ability of the selected vendor to share product knowledge and partner on appropriate industry strategies with us. Anybody can negotiate price, but I want a partner."

Wendy Imamura,
C.P.M., CPPB, CMIR,
Material Processing Center
Manager, Verizon Hawaii Inc.

"I'm familiar with these types of seminars. Chances are, if the seminar is truly objective and informative, that sales rep's company will be the first one we contact when looking for their type of product or service."

Kim Walker,
Facilities Manager,
Acordia Northwest Inc.

"When it comes to deciding on a new vendor, all things being equal, if one of them conducted useful and informative seminars, it would definitely help in influencing my decision."

Robert Click,
Purchasing Manager

"This type of service would definitely influence my decision since it is meaningful and helps build a solid relationship with the vendor."

Errol van Edema,
Manager of Purchasing &
Manufacturing/Distribution

"Purchasers like to be well-informed. A good supplier understands this and makes an effort to provide useful information resources to increase the value of the business relationship."

"There's a really good chance that I would read a postcard versus a letter. Postcards are easier to read and they quickly identify any key points. I think that this is a very effective method of direct mail."

— *HENRY VALIULUS, Director of Purchasing*

 **Secret 10**   *Customized Business Postcards*

Buyer's side of the desk: As a busy buyer, how likely is it that you would take the time to open and read all the unsolicited mail you received? There are just not enough hours in the day.

That's why we recommend that you supplement your follow-up with customized business postcards.

Scenario:
You have spoken with a prospect and determined they may need your product or service–not immediately, but sometime in the future.

While it's important to maintain contact, our buyers unanimously agreed that there was a fine line between keeping in touch with your prospects and annoying them. After three or four months of check-in calls, a call every month may cease to be effective and become unwelcome.

This presents a dilemma for the sales rep:

- Excessive follow up: annoy the buyer and lose the sale.

- Not enough follow up: be forgotten and lose the sale.

In situations like this, a creative or humorous postcard can be valuable. Using them to supplement your follow-up calls may increase your chances of getting business when the prospect is ready to buy.

Example: Marketshare needed a short-run printing of books, so we requested quotes from several suppliers. The proposals were followed up by calls, but by that time, our plans had been delayed. The only thing we could tell the reps was that we didn't know when we would need to run the job.

Four months later, we unexpectedly received an eye-catching postcard promoting short-run printing technology.

It had a picture of a forlorn-looking author slumped at her desk, surrounded by thousands of copies of her new book. The caption read, "Why hasn't Oprah called?"

This card caught our attention—but more to the point, the timing was impeccable, as we were now ready to go to print.

To create your own business postcard, all you need is an idea that shows your product or service solving a problem—or, as with the card in the example, an idea showing the pain caused by *not* using your product or service.

You can also use postcards to communicate your **Industry Specific Positioning Statement** (see *Secret 2).*

We asked the Buyers: What percentage of reps use postcards as marketing tools?

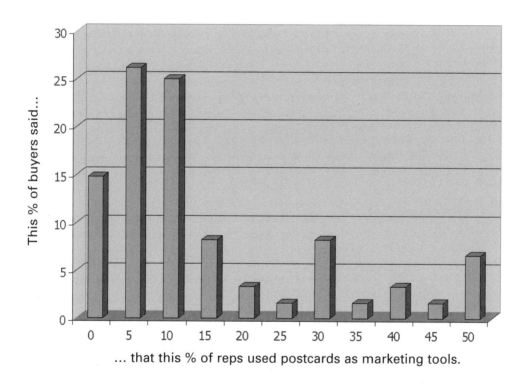

This % of buyers said...

... that this % of reps used postcards as marketing tools.

Summary: The vast majority of the buyers said that **less than 25% of reps used postcards** as marketing tools.

The Buyers Comment

Richard Lusk, *Director of Purchasing,* *Lennar Homes, Inc.*	"I typically open all mail. A postcard has the potential to be more effective because it is more compact and thus a quicker read. I can make a decision about its worth much more quickly. A brochure and letter tend to take more time, and if the material contains an introduction, body, and closing, then it may lose my attention. It must be brief so that I can skim it."
Peter Van der Hoek, *Buyer/Planner*	"I would probably read a postcard as they are usually more to the point. If it is of interest, then I would follow up and ask for more literature."
Charles Tobler, **C.P.M., MPP,** *Senior Buyer*	"I don't have time to read long sales letters. They would just get a glance. The same goes for the brochures unless they caught my eye for an immediate need. There would however, be about a 75 percent chance that I would read a postcard because they are small."
Kristen Mitchell, *Senior Buyer,* *Boston Financial Data* *Services Incorporated*	"Give an eye-catching summary and only use 'target words' in the copy."
Wm. Frank Quiett, **C.P.M., A.P.P.,** *Project Lead,* *Supply Chain Management* *and Strategic Sourcing*	"I receive flyers every day, and they just get pitched. The difference with a post card is that I will give it a quick look."

The Buyers Comment *cont'd*

Richard K. Tyler, C.P.M.,
Director of Purchasing, MRC Bearings

"If it is not addressed directly to me it will go straight to the trash. Be sure the mailing is addressed specifically to the person you wish to reach. Items addressed 'Attn: Purchasing Dept.' or 'Attn: Purchasing Mgr.' probably won't reach anyone. Many places have instructions in their mail-sorting areas to dispose of that type of mail immediately."

Brad Bigelow,
Manager of Purchasing and Vendor Relations

"I would look at it, if it were an interesting postcard. What I would really like to see is a postcard that incorporated a business card, with perforations to remove the card for future reference."

SECTION

2

PREPARING

Okay, you've set an appointment with a buyer or other decision-maker. Even if this person can't authorize the funds for your product or service, it's important to remember that they probably have the power to say "No." This could sabotage any of your future potential with this prospect.

No doubt you've heard the phrase, "You never get a second chance to make a good first impression." It's especially true with first sales meetings. The goal of this section is for you to arrive at your meeting feeling confident that you will make an outstanding first impression. If you want to differentiate yourself from competing sales reps, you're in the right place: Not only are these approaches Buyer-Approved, but—amazingly— most sales reps fail to use them.

Before I let you go, I'd like to leave you with this thought: Imagine you are going to perform in a professional play. Would you go onstage without learning your lines, and rehearsing them? True, you can't script a sales meeting in advance—but for that very reason, it's even more important to research your prospect; plan specific, effective approaches; and mentally prepare yourself by rehearsing likely scenarios. Only then can you maximize your chance of outperforming the competition.

Enjoy the read—and developing your questions, GPOS's, and other tools—and I'll talk to you in Section 3.

—Mike

"Credibility dissipates in front of your eyes. I won't trust their business and they won't get my business."

— *WAYNE NORDIN C.P.M., V.P. & Procurement Manager, Sun Trust Bank*

 **Secret 11** **Pre-Meeting Research**

The buyer's side of the desk: Can you imagine agreeing to meet with a sales rep, only to find they have no clue what your company does? It's hard to believe, but our buyers confirmed it: Too many sales reps arrive at first meetings thinking they have the right to waste the buyer's time with questions they could have answered with the most basic research!

So don't waste your prospect's time. Do your homework. The sales professionals who win key accounts usually do extensive research before meeting with prospects. While buyers may not always notice that you've done this extra research, they sure notice when you haven't!

Here are some questions you may want to find the answers to before the meeting:

- How many locations do they have, and is this the head office?

- Is the company private or public, and is there a parent company?

- Have they /are they acquiring any companies?

- Have they recently been in the news or had major publicity?

- Who are their competitors?

- Who are their major customers?

- Why do their customers buy from them?

- What is their annual revenue?

- When is their fiscal year-end?

- What are their main product/service lines?

- Has anyone in senior management been replaced recently?

- Are they in a budget freeze?

- What are their major challenges?

To help with your research, try Web search tools such as **www.google.com**, or **www.copernic.com**. In the case of a publicly-traded company, try **http://finance.yahoo.com**, where you can find information on a company's financials, employee counts, officers' names, and website links.

We asked the Buyers: On a scale of 1 to 10 (10 being highest), how important is it to you for a rep to do research prior to meeting with you?

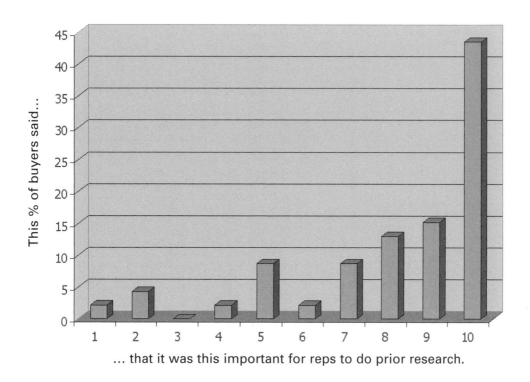

... that it was this important for reps to do prior research.

Summary: The vast majority of the buyers considered it **extremely important** for reps to do research prior to meetings.

We asked the Buyers: What percentage of reps seem to have done research prior to meeting with you?

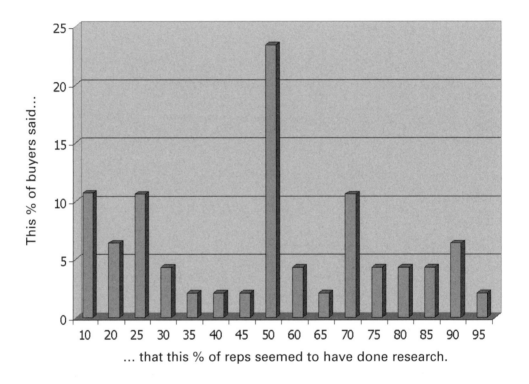

... that this % of reps seemed to have done research.

Summary: The majority of the buyers said that **most reps did not** seem to have done any research prior to their sales meetings.

The Buyers Comment

Sheryl Haeberle, *Buyer, Brigham Young University—Idaho*	"I do not do business with someone who has not taken the time to know about my business."
Judy Elrite, C.P.M., *Buyer Specialist*	"It has an extremely negative impact. If they are not interested enough to do research, they are not interested enough to be doing business on a long-term basis. I have no wish to deal with lazy salespeople. How can they help me if they know nothing about my company?"
Mike Kanze, **MBA, C.P.M., A.P.P.,** *President, Cornerstone Services Incorporated*	"*Big* negative. They've wasted my time, as I've probably had to explain things they could have found out about us in the public domain."
Joyce M. Knapp, **C.P.M.,** *Senior Buyer, Cooper Energy Services*	"It gives me a negative impression. I think of them as not being good salespeople. I would not be as likely to have another meeting with them."
Jim Haining, **C.P.M., A.P.P., MBA,** *Manager, Corporate Agreements for a leading telecommunications company*	"I generally turn them off quickly and terminate the meeting."

"Can you give me some key performance indicators defined by your company... as in measures of success that you've benchmarked against the industry to determine what you're doing well and what needs improvement?"

— *GREG TENNYSON, C.P.M., CPCM, Vice President, Corporate Procurement, Oracle Corporation*

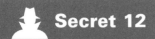 **Secret 12**   ## Tough Questions

The buyer's side of the desk: Imagine you're a buyer meeting with a sales rep. You're asking some tough questions that demand answers. The rep is doing a lot of hemming and hawing, or promising to "get back to you" about them. How much confidence in the sales rep does this give you?

No one can expect you to have all the answers all the time, but you can be ready for likely questions, and even some unlikely ones. Many sales reps have great verbal agility, but the best take the time to be sure their answers are as good as they can be. There's nothing worse than being put on the spot with a tough question and having to struggle for an answer.

Here are some tough questions buyers may ask:

- "I like your proposal, but the VP at our head office would make this decision. I'd like to promote it for you–how would you recommend I sell him on it?"

- "What metrics did you use to determine your projected results?"

- "How can I be sure that you'll honor your warranty?"

- "Let's say we're experiencing critical downtime with your product/service. How quickly can you get us up and running again? Can you give me an example of how you've handled this with other clients?"

- "Can you prove to us that your company is financially stable enough to honor the service warranty for the full term of the contract?"

Examples from the Buyers

Beckie Beard, **C.P.M, A.P.P, CACM,** *Director, Purchasing &* *Materials Management,* *Lansing Community College*	"What do you know about our needs for _____? How long have you been selling this product/service? (If less than a year:) Do you really know enough about it that I should listen to your advice?"
Chris Nield, *Corporate Buyer,* *International Truck* *and Engine Corp.*	"What differentiates your product from your competitor's? (I ask this of everyone in the first meeting.)"
Wm. Frank Quiett, **C.P.M., A.P.P.,** *Project Lead, Supply Chain* *Management and Strategic* *Sourcing*	"How can your company increase my effectiveness, reduce costs, or improve customer satisfaction?"
Grahame Gill, *Facilities Buyer*	"How can you help me save money?"
Jeff Hardman, *Director of Network* *Operations*	"What is the *value* in your product/service?"
Mike Kanze, **C.P.M., A.P.P., MBA,** *President & CEO,* *Cornerstone Services Inc.*	"Based on what you know about our firm, tell me why you think your product or service is right for us. (The answer to this question tells me a lot about how much the seller has looked at our business situation, and whether their offering meets a real need or is simply a 'hammer looking for a nail.')"

Examples from the Buyers *cont'd*

Dean R. Schlosser, Jr.,
Purchasing Agent

"What differentiates your product from similar products? (This moves the conversation toward the value-added services, like support staff, service department, and price. This question is very good, especially if the same equipment is supplied by different companies, under different names.)"

Gregory W. Hunter,
Manager of Purchasing, Cannon USA

"How can you improve my bottom line?"

Natalie Levy,
V.P. Divisional Merchandise Manager, Lord and Taylor

"Why do you think we will be successful if we choose your product?

Whom do you consider your competition?"

Steve Mataya,
Materials Manager, Allied Gear & Machine Co. Inc.

"What exactly will you do in terms of support and follow-through?"

Kenneth F. Esbin,
Purchasing Manager, Tarmac America

"What competitive advantage can you provide me?

How is your company preparing for the potential strike in the _____ industry?

What do you see the economy doing? I know what my indicators say, but what do *yours* say?"

Planning Guide: Take some time to write some other tough questions you think your prospect could ask—and your answers.

We asked the Buyers: What percentage of reps have trouble answering questions that you believe they should be prepared to answer?

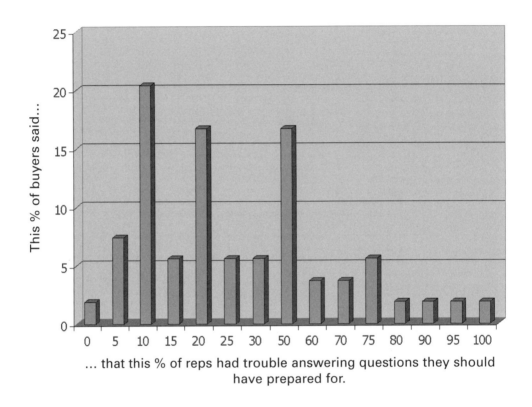

... that this % of reps had trouble answering questions they should have prepared for.

Summary: The majority of reps **had trouble answering questions** they should have prepared for.

Key Point for Sales Management

We asked the buyers if they had any favorite "tough" questions they like to ask reps in the first meeting. The one that kept coming up was:

Why is your company/product/service better than your competitors'?

It's crucial to decide on the best way to answer this. With that in mind, sales managers need to ask:

- Do all our sales reps answer this question the same way?

- If not, who does have the best answer?

- Shouldn't all our reps be using that answer?

One of the Buyers, **Peter Van der Hoek**, Buyer/ Planner, observed: "I find that some reps get baffled when you ask them what the advantages would be in dealing with them. I would hope they were prepared for that type of question, but I am amazed how many are not."

"It is rare for someone else to raise the objection first. It's unusual, but it's a very good idea."

— *BRIAN SMITH, Director of Inventory Management, Corporate Express*

 **Secret 13** | ### The Genuine Preemptive Objection Statement (GPOS)

The buyer's side of the desk: As a buyer, you would appreciate sales reps who demonstrated their preparedness and objectivity. Our research confirms that buyers prefer reps to handle objections proactively.

Does this sound familiar? You're making a presentation, and it's going well—until your prospect raises an objection. Suddenly your carefully-organized presentation has taken a 45-degree turn, and you're on the defensive.

It doesn't have to be that way. When you can anticipate your prospect's objections and address them in a positive and informative way, you can actually give your prospect some key insights and enhance your presentation.

That's the power of the Genuine Preemptive Objection Statement (GPOS). We emphasize the word *genuine*—a GPOS works only when it is logical and forthright.

For example, if the conversation turns to price, you can introduce the following GPOS *before* your prospect brings up a lower-priced competitor:

"Yes, let's talk about price for a moment. Our product/service is priced about 20% higher than most of our competitors'—yet we're signing new business all the time. And in every case, the reason people buy from us is value. You see, independent research confirms our product's lifespan is nearly double the industry standard. So you get double the value, yet you pay only 20% more."

Notice how the rep cited his company's high standards *without directly criticizing the competition*. This is part of the "positive" in GPOS; it shows confidence and integrity.

In this next example, you represent a small but fast-growing service provider. Your prospect has just complained about frequent service interruptions with their current provider. The prospect's next thought could be, "If XYZ MegaCorp. can't give us dependable service, how can you?" This is a chance to use a GPOS. You can preempt the objection by explaining that your company's size allows it to specialize and give *better* service than a larger, diversified company:

"John, we're one of the smallest providers in the city, so it made sense for us to focus on a particular market niche and become experts in it. That's allowed us to deliver 23% more up-time than the local industry average."

Once you become familiar with the GPOS concept, you will realize there are regular opportunities to use them in prospect meetings. The key is to have your GPOS rehearsed and ready, so you can notice when your conversation is heading for a likely objection. Remember, you're not *responding* to an objection, you're *anticipating* it. But even when your prospect objects before you can deliver your GPOS, you're ready to answer intelligently and positively.

Planning Guide: Make a list of objections that commonly occur during your presentations. Choose the objections that could provide your customers with key information, and write a GPOS for each.

We asked the Buyers: On a scale of 1 to 10 (10 being highest), how effective is it for reps to handle objections proactively and positively?

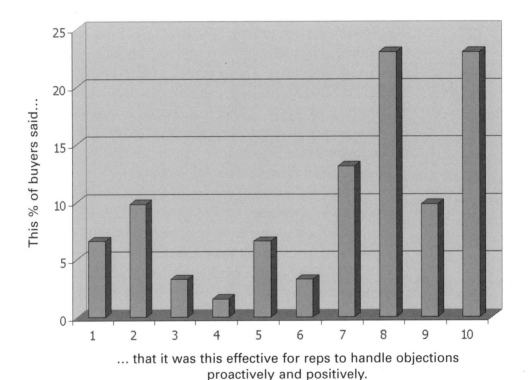

... that it was this effective for reps to handle objections proactively and positively.

Summary: The vast majority of the buyers felt it was **effective** when reps anticipated objections in a positive way.

We asked the Buyers: What percentage of reps handle objections proactively and positively?

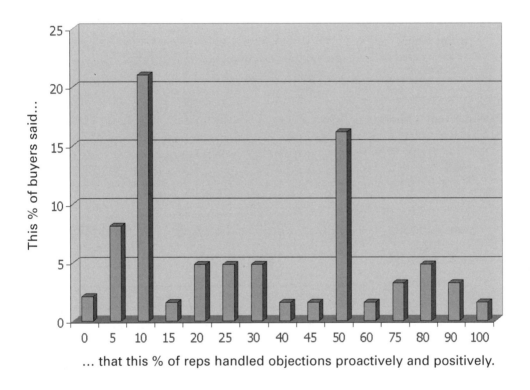

This % of buyers said...

... that this % of reps handled objections proactively and positively.

Summary: Almost half of the buyers had **rarely** seen reps handle objections this way.

The Buyers Comment

Edward DiLello, C.P.M., *Procurement Specialist,* *Philadelphia Gas Works*	"This kind of proactive approach indicates to me that the rep knows his/her organization, its strengths and weaknesses."
Brent Long, *Records Management* *Coordinator*	"This is a great idea, and it would save a lot of the beating around the bush that goes on regularly."
Wm. Frank Quiett, C.P.M., A.P.P., *Project Lead, Supply Chain* *Management and* *Strategic Sourcing*	"Once a customer raises an issue, it becomes an objection. By bringing it up first, the sales rep keeps the customer from seeing it as a negative obstacle."
Stan Marshall, C.P.M., *Purchasing Manager*	"It is always good to be proactive, and this definitely is."
Henry Valiulus, *Director of Purchasing*	"I think this a very good idea, as long as it is done sincerely and doesn't bash the competition. Many reps are well prepared to handle objections, but I've never experienced a rep presenting this in advance. It would save a lot of time."

 **Secret 14** **Effective Questions**

Buyer's side of the desk: As a buyer, you would appreciate sales reps who came to you with insightful questions that made you think about problems and solutions at a deeper level. This is what "consultative selling" means.

That said, some sales-training resources suggest you use a wide range of questioning techniques with names like

- Probing questions

- Porcupine questions

- Objection questions

- Leading questions

- Third party questions

- Comparative questions

- Developmental questions

- Presentation questions

- Motivation questions

A simpler approach might be to compile a list of questions to help you achieve your initial sales meeting objective:

To quickly determine if your product/service can help your prospect's company increase revenues or decrease expenses.

We recommend you prepare for each sales meeting by creating a list of key questions specific to your prospect. To help you with this, we have compiled some insightful questions from the following three sources.

Here are examples from Art Sobczak's book *How to Sell More in Less Time With No Rejection, Using Common Sense Telephone Techniques, Volume 1:*

- What kind of turnaround time do you really want, and what do you get now?

- How do you measure good service?

- How would you define a good value for your money?

- What was the criteria you used when you chose your present supplier?

- What were the determining factors in selecting the company you're now using?

- If you we able to design the perfect _____, what would it look like/do?

Consider starting questions with phrases such as

- When was the last time you needed to ...?

- What do you do when ...?

- How would you handle ...?

- What happens when ...?

Our thanks to Art Sobczak for allowing us to include this important material. You can reach Art at:

Business By Phone Inc.
13254 Stevens St.
Omaha, NE 68137
(402) 895-9399
www.businessbyphone.com

Jill Konrath shares some effective questions from her book *Winning More Sales: Take Your Business to the Next Level with Insightful, Powerful Questions:*

- From a _____ perspective, what are the biggest challenges your firm is facing today?

- What things are most important to your customers today?

- What are the greatest challenges your department faces in achieving its objectives?

- How do your problems with _____ prevent you from achieving your objectives?

- What's the Ripple Effect of the problem you described? What other areas are impacted?

- How do you measure success working with your current supplier?

- What are your criteria for establishing a new business relationship?

- If you determine that several companies meet your needs, what other criteria become important in your decision?

- Are you aware of any obstacles to us working together on this project?

Our thanks to Jill Konrath for allowing us to include this important material. You can reach Jill at:

Selling to Big Companies
2227 Foxtail Court
White Bear Lake, MN 55110
(651) 429-1922
www.sellingtobigcompanies.com

Some sample questions, courtesy of the buyers:

Trent N. Baker, **C.P.M.,** *Purchasing Manager,* *Wilson Foods, Division of* *Reser's Fine Foods, Inc.*	"What's the most important thing a supplier like us could do to help you and your company be more effective and profitable?"
Scott Bartel, *Sourcing Strategist*	"What do I need to do to help you compare your present vendor's offering versus mine?"
Lori Aljets, *Purchasing and Quality* *Assurance Manager, Norpac* *Foods Inc.*	"I want to exceed your expectations: How would you go about defining a good supplier?"
Grahame Gill, *Facilities Buyer*	"What do you look for when selecting a product/or service?"

We asked the Buyers: What percentage of reps ask you good questions on their sales calls?

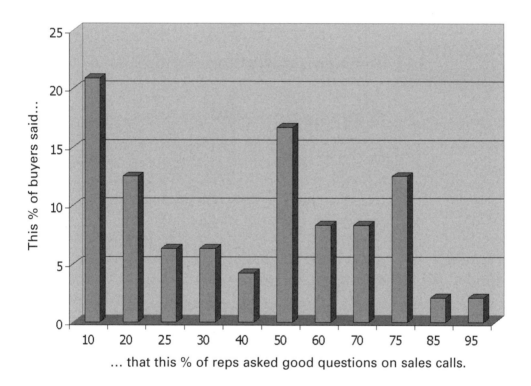

This % of buyers said....

... that this % of reps asked good questions on sales calls.

Summary: The majority of buyers said that **most reps did not** ask good questions on sales calls.

"This is a ten out of ten. Most sales reps spend 15 minutes of my time going over brochures and talking about their company whether I know about them or not. I really like the idea of a single-page synopsis of company information."

—*ANNE STILWELL, Director, Contract and Procurement Services, Fannie Mae*

 **Secret 15** **Company Information Sheet (CIS)**

Buyer's side of the desk: Our research shows that when it comes to presenting initial information on a sales call, "less is more." Buyers are often given pages and pages of information they don't have time to read. If they're not reading your printed material, does it matter how impressive it appears?

Planning Guide:

A good Company Information Sheet uses bullet points on a single page and should contain the following items:

- Your ISPS or your PRS (See pages 4 or 9)

- Years in business

- An example of how your company gave ROI to a client in the prospect's industry

- A partial list of current clients—ideally, twelve clients in the prospect's industry. (See Secret 20 to expand on this item)

- Any relevant company certifications or awards

The Buyers Comment

Gene Roberts,
Manager of Purchasing

"Most reps send pages and pages of information about their company, and I don't have time for that. If they're doing a cold call or trying to introduce their company, they should have the one-page summary. They should all be using this approach, but I've never met one who does."

Leslie Champion,
Senior Procurement Specialist, Industrial Design & Construction, Inc.

"It's a good idea. Short bullet points and a single page are more likely to be read than pages of data about your company."

Roy Sekigawa,
Purchasing Operations Manager, Foremost Dairies, Hawaii

"I first saw one last week. It's useful for comments and feedback as well. Only a small percentage of reps use this type of sales tool, and I'd like to see more of them. I'd give this a nine out of ten."

Wendy Imamura, C.P.M., CPPB, CMIR,
Material Processing Center Manager, Verizon Hawaii Inc.

"I think a company information sheet is helpful. Take care to ensure that information is constantly updated. It is not worthwhile to spend a lot on glossy printing and volume, since dated material would look worse than no material!"

Jason Wihnon,
Supply Purchaser

"This is a nine out of ten since it would be a valuable sales aid. In ten years of purchasing I haven't seen one, but it's a great idea."

Angel Tutor,
Purchasing Coordinator, Wackenhut

"I think this is an excellent idea that very few reps use. I like this a lot."

"Unfortunately, only about 10 percent of my suppliers follow this procedure. If I could receive a schedule prior to the meeting and remove any content that would not be advantageous to me, it would certainly help the supplier, who could then spend more time on issues of interest to me."

— *CHRISTOPHER LOCKE, Global Lead Buyer, DaimlerChrysler Corporation*

 **Secret 16**   **The Advance Meeting Agenda (AMA)**

Buyer's side of the desk: Meetings are part of business life—yet far too many of them consume unnecessary time because they lack structure. As a buyer, would you have more confidence in a sales rep who sent you an agenda in advance of every meeting, or with one who just showed up and "winged it"?

That's why we strongly suggest that, prior to each meeting, you email your prospect an Advance Meeting Agenda and invite their changes to it.

An agenda should chronologically list your meeting's key topics. When you email your prospect an Advance Meeting Agenda, you

- Show respect for the prospect's time, and your interest in addressing the company's needs.

- Learn more about the company's needs and are able to prepare for them.

- Let the prospect feel more involved in the meeting process.

- Let the prospect prepare any required information.

- Show you have done your "homework" researching the company.

- Show that you are proactive, organized and competent.

Example: ***Advance Meeting Agenda:*** Here's an example of an email message containing an AMA. (In the example, "BuyerCo." is the buyer's company; "ABC Co." is the sales rep's company.)

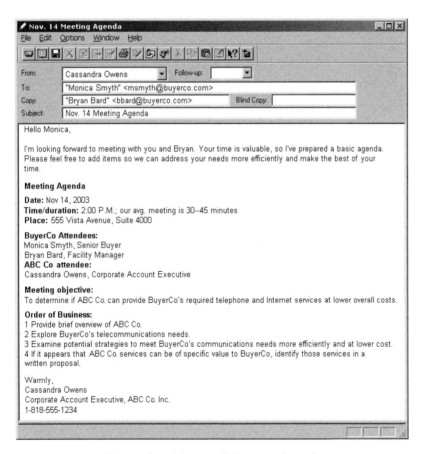

Example: Advance Meeting Agenda

We asked the Buyers: On a scale of 1 to 10 (10 being highest), how important is it for reps to prepare a meeting agenda in advance?

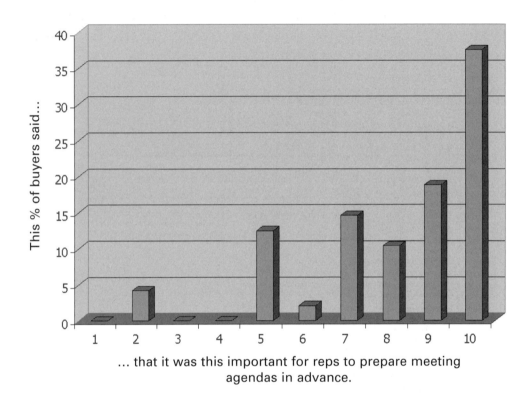

... that it was this important for reps to prepare meeting agendas in advance.

Summary: 80% of buyers felt it was **extremely important** for reps to prepare meeting agendas in advance.

The Buyers Comment

Wm. Frank Quiett,
C.P.M., A.P.P.,
Project Lead,
Supply Chain Management
and Strategic Sourcing

"The proposed agenda gives the buyer/manager something with which to compare his requirement/interest, and allows him to share the proposed agenda with colleagues, management, and cross-functional teams. Also—and this is important—it gives him/her the opportunity to adjust the meeting to meet a specific interest, prior to the meeting taking place. Actually, I would recommend that the letter [ask the buyer to] respond with 'Yes, this is fine,' or 'I would like to recommend …' Either way, you are getting 'buy-in' up-front… a major step in drawing the buyer and putting substance into the meeting."

Toni Horn, C.P.M.,
Global Commodity Manager,
Silicon Graphics Inc.

"It is easier to set up the attendee list when you have an agenda. It also allows for adding to the agenda or removing what you don't want. At my company, no one has time to spend on meetings that do not specifically address their needs."

Natalie Levy,
V.P. Divisional Merchandise
Manager, Lord and Taylor

"I think it's great to know what the topics will be before the meeting. It shows that the sales rep is serious and prepared for the meeting."

Stan Marshall, C.P.M.,
Purchasing Manager

"It helps define the time period that will be needed for the meeting and the areas which have to be covered. If there is no need to cover a particular area due to current agreements, this reduces the waste of our time."

The Buyers Comment *cont'd*

Lori Aljets, *Purchasing and Quality Assurance Manager, Norpac Foods Inc.*	"It suggests an organized, educated, interested company."
Richard Lusk, **C.P.M., CPPB, CMIR,** *Material Processing Center Manager, Verizon Hawaii Inc.*	"It would cut to the chase and prepare the participants for a direct and pointed meeting."
Mike Kanze, **C.P.M., A.P.P., MBA,** *President & CEO, Cornerstone Services Inc.*	"Presented sufficiently in advance, it gives the buyer the opportunity to reject inappropriate agenda points or change them accordingly. It also forces the vendor to think rationally in advance about the meeting and to set realistic goals about the meeting's outcome."
Lynda Stewart, *General Manager, Praga Industries Co. Ltd.*	"It verifies and confirms the appointment and gives the buyer an opportunity to prepare the required information and/or to make changes."
Jim Morey, *Vice President of Procurement, Sara Lee Foods, a division of Sara Lee Corporation*	"This is pretty important—it helps to keep you on track in the meeting, and it makes things much more efficient."
Dusty Rhoads, C.P.M., *Contract Administrator, First Energy Corporation*	"It's important—a ten out of ten—[but] only if the rep has done their homework and the agenda contains relevant, to-the-point bullets."

Key Point for Sales Management

When two or more company representatives team up for a sales meeting, it's important for them to plan and rehearse their presentation to ensure a seamless and professional delivery.

Planning Guide:

- How will the agenda items be divided?

- Who will answer questions about service, price, warranty, and other specific topics?

- Who will answer any unanticipated or sensitive questions?

The Buyers Comment

Ronald D. Ewen,
Purchasing Agent &
Assistant Projects Manager

"Usually, when meeting with two reps from the selling company, one is a superior of the other (like a sales manager and a sales rep). One tends to be more dominating (usually the sales manager), and the other, more intimidated by the situation. They don't act as a team at all. In my experience, this happens 100 percent of the time."

Anonymous

"When two representatives are meeting with me, they sometimes interrupt each other when responding to my questions, or they have conflicting answers. This does not instill confidence in the buyer."

We asked the Buyers: What percentage of rep teams are clearly unprepared when they meet with you?

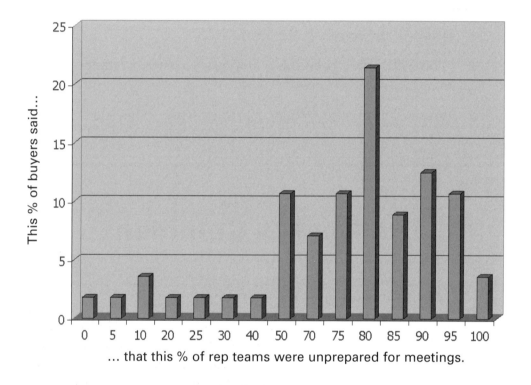

… that this % of rep teams were unprepared for meetings.

Summary: The vast majority of buyers said that **most rep teams were clearly unprepared** for meetings.

MEETING

Here it is, the Moment of Truth: The buyer or decision-maker greets you in the lobby of their business and invites you into their office. You've done your best to prepare yourself, you've rehearsed your meeting, and you feel confident. Your confidence is "contagious"—it tells the buyer you can do business proactively, competently, and professionally.

You are ready to show the buyer that you can make their job easier by

- Quickly determining if you offer something the buyer needs; and, if so,

- Presenting your information accurately and efficiently.

The goal of this section is to have you leave your sales meeting feeling confident that you have communicated clearly; that you have "covered all the bases" in a structured, effective way; and that you are on your way to developing trust.

Enjoy the read, and creating your meeting planner. I'll talk to you in Section 4.

—Mike

"It makes sense for sales reps to start off with a brief introduction of their company. I can't tell them what my needs are until I know what they can offer."

— *BRIAN MORAN, Director Americas' Supply Management, Siemens Westinghouse Power Corporation*

Secret 17   Company Overview

Buyer's side of the desk: You're a buyer, and you're having a first meeting with a sales rep from a company you'd never heard of. The rep begins the meeting by asking probing questions about your business without first establishing his or her credibility. How does this make you feel?

It's important to map out your sales-meeting strategy, but pay close attention to respect and courtesy. For example, *earn the right to ask your prospect questions by first establishing your credibility*. The idea is not to sell, but to give the buyer enough information to make them comfortable about continuing the conversation. We recommend the following approach:

Planning Guide:

- State your ISPS or PRS (See pages 4 or 9).

- Name a few of your key accounts.

- Using the example from your Company Information Sheet, briefly describe how your company provided ROI to a client in the prospect's industry.

■ Give the prospect a printed copy of your Company Information Sheet (see *Secret 15*).

Example: "Monica, before we get into the meeting, I was hoping I could share a few key points about [my company]. Would that be ok?

"We specialize in reducing minimum billing costs for the call-center industry. We've worked with XYZ Call Co. and CBD Calling for You Co., two of the largest centers in the US. In fact, XYZ Call Co. selected us out of five vendors, and we've been saving them 30% a month ever since. May I leave this company information sheet with you? Great. Now may I ask you a few questions about [your company]?"

 **Secret 18** **The Meeting Planner**

You have finally connected with an elusive key prospect. You asked the right questions, you said the right things, and you got the appointment. The prospect made it clear you were the last of five suppliers they were considering. But you've done your homework, and you've prepared your *meeting planner*—a tool designed to ensure that your meeting goes smoothly and effectively.

Meeting Planner Components

The meeting planner is simply a binder or folder that organizes the items you need for a successful meeting. It consists of a checklist and appropriate supporting documents, all of which are covered in this book.

Sample Checklist:

Meeting agenda	_____	(page 60)
Company overview	_____	(page 69)
Company information sheet	_____	(page 58)
Questions	_____	(page 54)
Proposal required?	_____	
References	_____	(page 78)
Summarize key points and action items	_____	(page 86)
Post meeting: Send email summary	_____	(page 133)
Prepare proposal	_____	(page 93)

Document Checklist:

Copy of Email agenda	_____	(page 60)
Company information sheet	_____	(page 58)
Question sheet	_____	(page 53)
Answers to potential questions	_____	(page 42)
Company research sheet	_____	(page 37)
Critical questions sheet	_____	(page 74)

We asked the Buyers: What percentage of reps are clearly unprepared for the sales call and have apparently not planned a meeting structure?

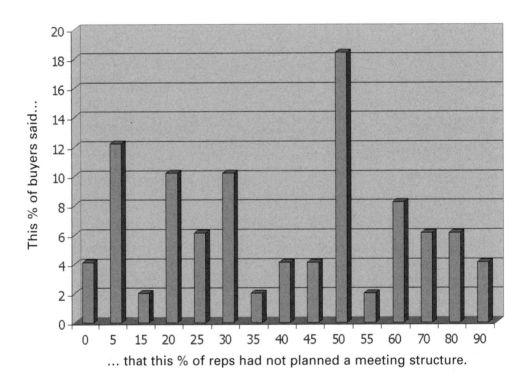

... that this % of reps had not planned a meeting structure.

Summary: The majority of buyers said that **only about 1 in 2 reps** arrived with a prepared meeting structure.

"Implying that they understand your problems and have the willingness to answer questions about their competitors shows confidence in their company, products, and their ability to understand the industry. That is very important to me."

— *DAVID MIZER, Vice President Strategic Sourcing, Carnival Cruise Lines Inc.*

 **Secret 19** | **Objective Questions**

Buyer's side of the desk: You've just had an initial meeting with a new rep. The rep left you with some objective questions that you could ask all potential vendors—some of which you had not considered, but which were intrinsic to a sound buying decision. Does that increase your confidence in the rep's ability to serve your needs?

Our research shows that buyers appreciate it when reps leave them with objective questions for vendors; they consider it "extra value" before the sale. By providing some important questions the buyer might not have considered, you can help the buyer make a more informed decision.

At the end of the sales meeting, you can introduce your list of questions this way: "Monica, I've put together a few questions that might be helpful in making your decision. They're objective questions that you should ask any vendor before you decide to move forward. May I leave them with you?"

Questions for Vendors

- What happens if you can't run our advertisements in the promised timeslots?

- How do you measure the results of the training, and what kind of retention do you guarantee?

- What happens if you can't honor your service response-time guarantee?

- What happens if replacement parts are discontinued?

- What contingency plan do you have for downtime?

- Do you have tracking reports I can access online?

- What happens if we have an equipment failure? Does your company provide a loaner? If so, does it cost anything?

- When you service our equipment, do you use new or refurbished parts?

- Do you actively recycle your discarded parts, and do you have other environmental policies?

Planning Guide: Create your own list of objective questions critical to the buyer's decision.

The Buyers Comment

Greg Graham, *Buyer, Kenworth Truck Company*	"Interesting idea, I've never seen anyone do it. I think the questions would have to be objective in order for it to be effective."
Kristen Mitchell, *Senior Buyer, Boston Financial Data Services Incorporated*	"This could be very helpful, but be careful not to put down competitors in an effort to make your company look better. The right questions should be indicators that the seller has confidence that his/her company has the preferred response."
Lynda Stewart, *General Manager, Praga Industries Co. Ltd.*	"If these questions were made available, I think they would have some value in the decision making process."
Richard Lusk, *Director of Purchasing, Lennar Homes, Inc.*	"Maybe they will bring up something we haven't considered. That would be helpful for us."
Edward DiLello, C.P.M., *Procurement Specialist, Philadelphia Gas Works*	"This would be valuable because different reps bring different experiences and perspectives to the table. Situations may have occurred elsewhere that have not occurred [yet] in the buyer's organization."

We asked the Buyers: At the end of a sales meeting, if a rep left you with two or three objective questions to ask other vendors—questions that would help you make the best buying decision— how valuable would that be on a scale of 1 to 10 (10 being highest)?

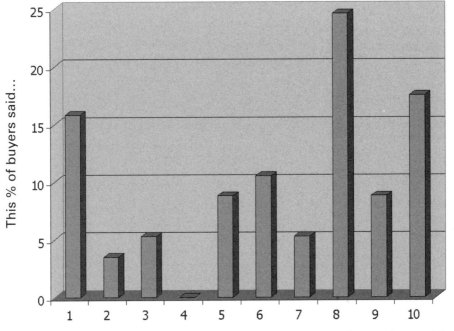

... that it would be this valuable for reps to leave them with two or three objective questions for other vendors.

Summary: The majority of buyers felt that objective questions were **very valuable** to an informed purchase decision.

We asked the Buyers: How many reps leave you with objective questions that can be critical to your purchasing decisions?

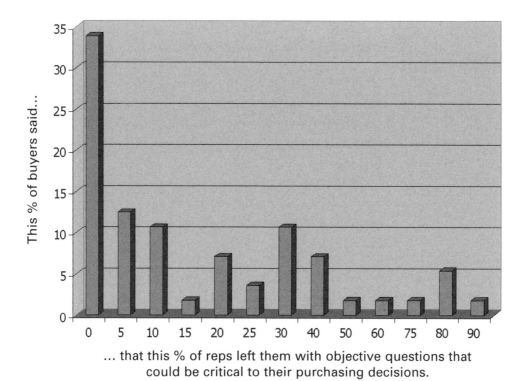

... that this % of reps left them with objective questions that could be critical to their purchasing decisions.

Summary: The majority of buyers had **rarely, if ever,** seen reps use this approach.

"A testimonial letter on its own rates a two out of ten. The value of references which we can call would be a ten out of ten."

— JIM MOREY, Vice President-Procurement,
Sara Lee Foods, a division of Sara Lee Corporation

 **Secret 20**   **Industry-Specific References**

It's a common belief that glowing testimonial letters can help influence a sale. But think about it: Have you ever read a *bad* testimonial? How useful are they as a sales tool?

When we interviewed our buyers, we found that they valued testimonial letters much less than they did *appropriate* references with whom they could *speak directly*. In general

■ Buyers felt that testimonial letters had little or no impact on their decisions.

■ Buyers felt that appropriate, live references had significant influence on their decisions.

Scenario:
You're in an initial sales meeting. You've determined there is a fit, and the prospect has asked you to prepare a proposal. As you're summarizing the requirements for the proposal, you offer the prospect the opportunity to call three of the clients on your Company Information Sheet (Secret 15, page 58). You invite them to select any three clients, and tell them you will include the contact information for these references in your proposal.

For each client on your reference page, include

- The references' contact information

- Their products/services

- The number of years they have been your client

- A brief description of how your reference benefited from doing business with you.

Example: *Client Reference Page*

Client: XYZ Co., Mark Smith, V.P. of Procurement. (888) 888-8888.

Industry: Call Centers

Years as client: 3

Service Provided: Long-Distance

Benefit to client: We saved XYZ Co. $10,000 over the last 3 years, with no downtime.

The Buyers Comment

Toni Horn, C.P.M.,
Global Commodity Manager,
Silicon Graphics Inc.

"Testimonial letters or awards from other customers alone do not impress me. The above approach would be very effective in gaining my business."

David Frieder,
Purchasing Director,
Planet Automotive Group Inc.

"I would want references from people who are in my field and who have related needs. I'm not interested in a reference from someone whose needs are different from mine."

Jim Haining,
C.P.M., A.P.P., MBA,
Manager, Corporate
Agreements for a leading
telecommunications company

"Forget the testimonial letters and give me references that I can call and question directly."

Judy Elrite, C.P.M.,
Buyer Specialist

"I much prefer talking to references and asking them questions directly. They need to be references that have something in common with my company or industry."

Erik Schlichting,
Inventory Control Manager

"If I cannot call and confirm a current level of satisfaction, they mean almost nothing."

Richard Lusk,
Director of Purchasing,
Lennar Homes, Inc.

"I always ask for references when going through the vendor-selection process. Testimonials with call info would be well-received."

Michael Tator,
V.P., Director of Production,
Wunderman, of the
Y & R Companies, Irvine

"I require the option of being able to telephone past clients–which I do follow up on. There are always production-related questions that I need to ask that are not covered in the letters and testimonials."

The Buyers Comment *cont'd*

Carl Colasurdo,
Director of Purchasing

"I have yet to receive a testimonial or letter of recommendation that made me want to deal with a specific vendor. I would probably be more impressed if I were handed a binder of letters from past customers that complained about the lousy service and high prices that the vendor provided—and if the representative then explained how the company resolved those issues and moved to a higher level through this customer criticism. Getting all the *happy guys* to write letters is of little value."

"It is very important for the rep to make sure he has answered the question completely. If not, it could pose expensive problems in the future—for both of us."

— *PAULA L. MARTIN, Corporate IT Buyer*

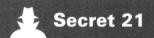 **Secret 21**   ## Complex Questions

Assume responsibility for clear communications by making sure that you've properly answered complex questions. In the natural flow of conversation, it's easy to move past one issue and jump into the next without any guarantee that both parties are "on the same page." Instead, confirm that your prospect understands by asking:

"Did I explain that clearly enough?"
Do not ask, "Did *you* get that okay?"

Example: ### *Confirming your response*

Prospect: I'm concerned about having users in different locations accessing the network. We have seven locations, and each location has twelve stations. Taking into account our need for maximum reliability and uptime, my question is, "How many users per location can access the network and how many total locations can we integrate?"

Sales rep: Our reliability is 100% guaranteed. Over 5000 clients are using our service, and none has ever had less than 98% uptime. Also, with our advanced system, up to 200 users can simultaneously access the network from up to ten remote locations. Each location allows a maximum of 20 users.

[Sales rep continues:] Monica, I just want to make sure I understood your question. Did I explain that clearly enough?

We asked the Buyers: On a scale of 1 to 10 (10 being highest), how important is it to you for a rep to confirm replies to your complex question?

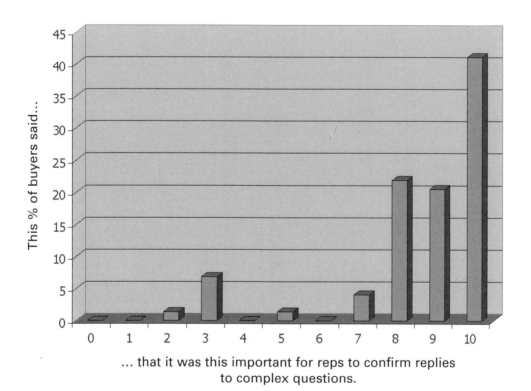

... that it was this important for reps to confirm replies to complex questions.

Summary: 85% of the buyers considered it **very important** for reps to confirm that they had clearly answered complex questions.

We asked the Buyers: What percentage of reps confirm their replies to complex questions?

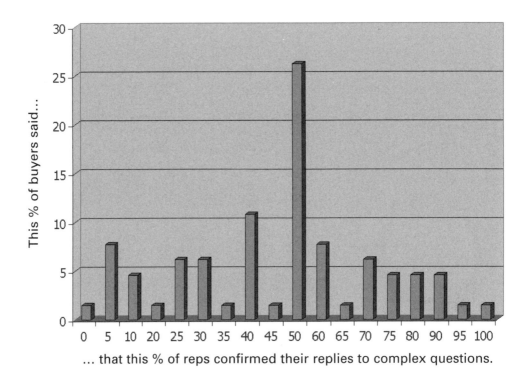

... that this % of reps confirmed their replies to complex questions.

Summary: The majority of buyers said that **less than half** of reps took the time to be sure they had answered complex questions clearly.

The Buyers Comment

Don Walraven,
Director of Inventory Management,
Alaska Distributors Co.

"This makes sense. It's important to make sure that both sides fully understand what is being said or agreed."

Sheryl Haeberle,
Buyer, Brigham Young University—Idaho

"It is extremely important to confirm understanding when the questions are complex."

Joe Hoffman,
Commodity Manager III

"It is extremely important that reps check to see if they handled questions properly."

Wendy Imamura,
C.P.M., CPPB, CMIR,
Material Processing Center Manager,
Verizon Hawaii Inc.

"Confirmation questions should be asked by the salesperson just in case the prospect is not comfortable about asking the same question over and over. The salesperson should also be trained in giving multiple examples to stress a point."

Wm. Frank Quiett,
C.P.M., A.P.P., *Project Lead,*
Supply Chain Management and Strategic Sourcing

"Making sure that questions are clearly understood is critical to the continuing relationship that the rep and the customer are trying to build."

Errol van Edema,
Manager of Purchasing & Manufacturing/Distribution

"Quality of information is paramount in the purchaser's work. Purchasers rely on the information provided by the reps, and that information flows to our internal customers. The rep's information and accuracy reflects on the buying organization."

"When you conclude a meeting, it makes sense to confirm the key points discussed. It's important that all parties are confident that real communication has taken place. A concise summary is an ideal way to achieve this goal."

— *ANDREW JULES DEGIULIO, Purchasing Manager*

 **Secret 22**   **Verbal Key Point Summary**

Buyer's side of the desk: You are a buyer. As you meet with reps, they fail to take notes or to summarize key action items with specific completion dates. When these items come up, they just say, "No problem, I'll take care of that"—and they don't. When you call them about it later, they say they simply forgot. Do you find this frustrating?

At the close of the meeting, summarize the key points you discussed to ensure that you and your prospect are on the "same page." An example:

"Monica, just to make sure I haven't missed anything, I'd like to recap the key points of our meeting: Tomorrow morning, I'm going to call Tracy Jackson to find out how much of your monthly long-distance is affected by the current 1-minute minimum, then I'll put together a written comparison which will compare what you're currently paying with our 3-second minimum billing format. I'll have the comparison in your email inbox by 3 P.M. tomorrow.

Then on Thursday I will meet with Kevin Lee, your operations manager, at your branch office in Richmond and conduct the same review I did with Tracy.

And by Friday, at 3 P.M., I'll have a proposal at your office, which will include the required hardware costs.

Does that cover everything, or is there anything I might have missed?"

Note to reader: When appropriate, summarize key points at the end of a telephone call as well.

We asked the Buyers: What percentage of reps summarize the key points you discussed during your meeting?

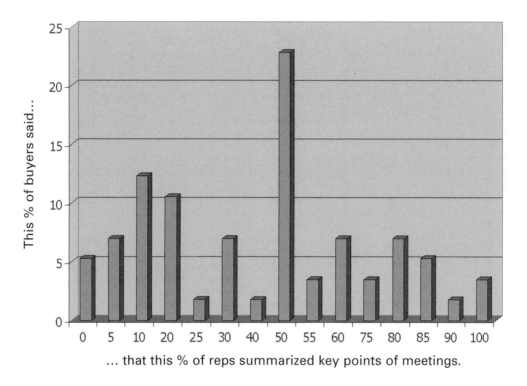

... that this % of reps summarized key points of meetings.

Summary: 46 % of the buyers said that the majority of reps **neglect to summarize** the key points of a meeting.

We asked the Buyers: On a scale of 1 to 10 (10 being highest), how important is it to you when a rep summarizes the key points of your meeting?

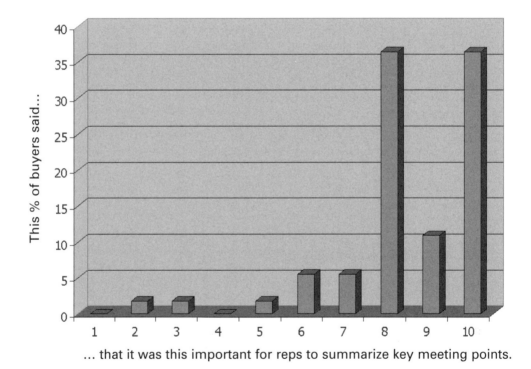

... that it was this important for reps to summarize key meeting points.

Summary: Over 80% of the buyers felt that summarizing a meeting's key points was **extremely important**.

The Buyers Comment

Lynne E. Gehrke,
Vice President, Procurement,
A. B. Dick Company

"Summarizing at the end of a meeting has great value. If I were to do sales training, this is one of the top skills I would definitely teach. It keeps both sides on track and becomes a very effective tool when confirmed via email. I use it today as an action item checklist."

Natalie Levy,
V.P./ Divisional Merchandise
Manager, Lord and Taylor

"This summarizing step is necessary so all parties are clear on how to proceed."

Stacey J. Zetterlund,
Supervisor, Direct Material
Sourcing, MRC Bearings

"If the rep doesn't summarize the key points and list the action items, then I do."

Mike Kanze,
C.P.M., A.P.P., MBA,
President & CEO,
Cornerstone Services Inc.

"This is an important step. Often, I'm the one who summarizes, because the rep forgets."

Kenneth F. Esbin,
Purchasing Manager,
Tarmac America

"Only about five to ten percent of the people I meet with actually make sure that we've communicated clearly on all points. It's important to summarize what was discussed and identify what the next steps are."

Peggy Jones,
Operations/H.R. Director,
Magic Software Enterprises, Inc.

"Summarizing key points gives me a chance to confirm expectations from the meeting and allows me to respond with any additions or changes I might have."

PROPOSING

Larger opportunities are often more complex and require more detailed proposals. The strategic proposal is the gateway to these big deals. The goal of this section is to provide you with a structure for preparing these complex proposals.

Keep in mind that strategic proposals are not necessary for all sales. Use shorter proposals when appropriate—but be sure to present them on your letterhead, not on the back of a brochure or on a fax cover page (as I have seen before!).

Enjoy the section. See you in a bit.

—Mike

"The proposal is important when determining which vendors should be short-listed. When certain buying decisions are shared, a properly detailed proposal is valuable because it addresses the concerns of all the departments involved."

— *DEAN R. SCHLOSSER, JR., Purchasing Agent*

 **Secret 23** ## The Strategic Proposal

Your planning and preparation paid off with a well-orchestrated meeting. You asked the right questions, said the right things, and confirmed an opportunity to help the buyer increase revenues. Your prospect has requested a proposal—you're on the short-list.

When it comes to creating proposals, many companies use preset formats that suit most selling situations. For more complex sales, consider a strategic proposal.

We are fortunate to have the contribution of a recognized expert in sales proposals, Robert F. Kantin. Bob is President of SalesProposals.com, and the author of several books on sales proposals, including *Sales Proposals Kit for Dummies*.

Here is an excerpt from Bob's book, *Strategic Proposals: Closing the Big Deal:*

Sales professionals may do everything right during the sale, but if they don't integrate the development of a strong, strategic proposal into the process, they put their sales at risk.

Strategic Proposal Structure

A strategic proposal contains five main sections. These sections are interrelated and customer-focused. They categorize information and provide a logical sequence of information and ideas.

1. **Background Information** identifies the buyer's current situation, the improvement opportunity—the buyer's unresolved problem or unachieved opportunity, and the basis for the proposal. Some recommended Section I subsections include

   - Industry Background

   - Client/Customer Background

   - Current Operations or Functions

   - Improvement Opportunity [Definition, Analysis, and Plans]

   - Client/Customer Needs and Objectives

   - Purpose of This Proposal

2. **Proposed Business Solution** presents the seller's proposed custom application of their products or services, and details how the seller will help the buyer achieve the improvement opportunity. Section II of a strategic proposal should contain four recommended subsections:

   ■ Product or Service Description

   ■ Product of Service Application

   ■ Non-financial (Qualitative) Benefits

   ■ Financial (Quantitative) Benefits

3. **Implementation Management** Section 3 presents the seller's implementation methodology or project management practices and schedules to assure the buyer that the seller is able to deliver on the contract.

   Like the first two strategic proposal sections that have definite subsection requirements, the third proposal section has three recommended subsections:

   ■ *Methods:* implementation, project, engagement, or management methods (or practices)

   ■ *Team:* implementation, project, engagement, or client service team

   ■ *Schedule:* implementation, project, or engagement schedule

4. **Seller Profile** discusses the seller's qualifications and business practices to further assure the buyer that the seller will be able to deliver on the contract and provide ongoing service.

   This section has six suggested subsections:

   - Mission or Customer Service Philosophy Statement

   - Company or Corporate Overview

   - Quality

   - Customer References

   - Why us?

   - Design and Development Checklist

5. **Business Issues** Section 5 profiles the seller's business and groups all business-related items for ease of review and reference, such as fees/prices, assumptions used for scheduling and pricing expenses, and when and how the seller will invoice the buyer.

6. **Most sellers** will find that three subsections suffice in the last strategic proposal section:

   - Assumptions: i.e. to adhere to the implementation schedule, a software development consultant might assume the buyer will review and approve design documents within five business days of receipt.

   - Fees/Prices and Other Expenses

   - Invoicing Schedule

Proposal Components

Additionally, a strategic proposal should include the following components:

- **Title Page**

- **Executive Summary**—as its name implies, a concise synopsis of the entire proposal

- **Table of Contents**—a listing of main sections and subsections with page numbers

- **Appendices**—used to support information contained in the main proposal sections; a place for preprinted forms, detailed financial calculations, product specifications, etc.

Use Appendices for Preprinted Materials

The overall appearance of a proposal is ruined when the seller includes preprinted materials in main proposal sections. Preprinted materials will interrupt a proposal's flow of information and ideas. Often when a writer puts a brochure or specifications sheet in the middle of a proposal section, he or she wants the recipient to find critical information in the document. The recipient would be better served if the seller summarized the information in one or two paragraphs and used the preprinted material as a supporting appendix.

Proposal Structure at a Glance

Executive Summary

I. Background Information
   a. Industry Information
   b. Background

> c. *Current Operation or Functions*
> d. *Improvement Opportunity [definition, analysis, and plans]*
> e. *Needs and Objectives [buyer]*
> f. *Purpose of this Proposal*

II. Proposed Solution
   a. *Product or Service Description*
   b. *Product or Service Application (optional)*
   c. *Nonfinancial Benefits*
   d. *Financial Benefits*

III. Implementation
   a. *Engagement or Project Management Methods*
   b. *Schedule*
   c. *Team*

IV. Seller Profile
   a. *Mission Statement*
   b. *Company Profile*
   c. *Quality*
   d. *Why Us?*
   e. *Other subsections based on the seller's industry or profession*

VI. Business Issues
   a. *Assumptions*
   b. *Fees/Prices [and other expenses]*
   c. *Invoicing Schedule*

Appendices

Our thanks to Bob Kantin for allowing us to include this important material. You can reach Bob at:

SalesProposals.com
2600 Ventura Drive, Suite 13210
Plano, TX 75093
(972) 612-4160
www.salesproposals.com

We asked the Buyers: What percentage of reps provide you with quality proposals?

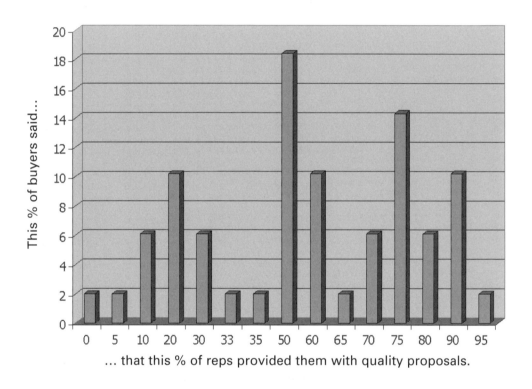

... that this % of reps provided them with quality proposals.

Summary: 45% of the buyers said only **about one in two reps** provide quality proposals.

We asked the Buyers: On a scale of 1 to 10 (10 being highest), how important is the quality of the sales proposal when you decide if you will give a vendor your business?

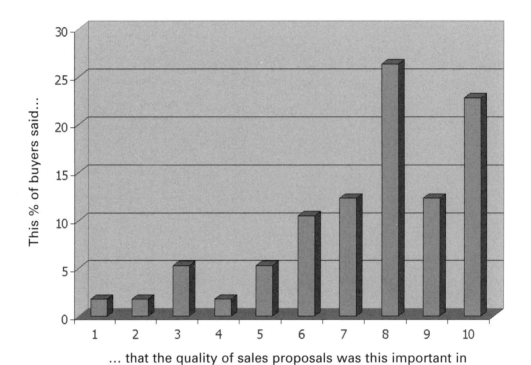

... that the quality of sales proposals was this important in influencing their buying decisions.

Summary: Over 75% of the buyers felt that the quality of proposals **influenced their buying decisions.**

The Buyers Comment

Kristen Mitchell, *Senior Buyer,* *Boston Financial Data* *Services Incorporated*	"Proposals are *very* important as they help us create a short list of the top two or three vendors. These vendors get the opportunity to come in and do a formal presentation."
Greg Tennyson, **C.P.M., CPCM,** *Vice President, Corporate* *Procurement,* *Oracle Corporation*	"The proposal is very important—a nine or ten out of ten. The proposal provides an opportunity for sales reps to do their homework, demonstrate their knowledge, and clearly articulate their value proposition to our buying group."
Peggy Jones, *Operations/H.R. Director,* *Magic Software Enterprises, Inc.*	"Proposals are very important, and most of the ones I receive are well done. A comprehensive proposal is a good way to demonstrate that you've done your homework."
Kenneth F. Esbin, *Purchasing Manager,* *Tarmac America*	"A good proposal tells me a great deal about the company's professionalism. If they have a professional presentation, it tells me they care about their company's perception in the marketplace."
Larry Stanley, *Senior Supply Chain Analyst*	"In terms of importance, this is definitely a ten out of ten. At our company, an incomplete proposal won't even be considered."
Krysia Diaz, CEBS, *Benefits Supervisor*	"Approximately 50% of the proposals I receive are of high quality. We recently received a couple that were really, really well done. They did an excellent job in giving us the exact information we wanted. When you get that kind of response, it makes it that much easier for you to lean to one side or the other. When you're dealing with two vendors and haven't decided which one to choose, extra effort in this area may tip the scales in the favor of one vendor."

CLOSING

Many sales reps think they must use clever closing approaches. But closing is more about the journey than the destination. If you've presented your information well, communicated clearly, and determined that a sale is in the buyer's best interests, closing should be simple and straightforward.

That is why this is the shortest section in the book. The goal of this section is to give you a well-deserved break—it shouldn't take much of your time.

Up to this point, you've researched and cold-called and researched some more and prepared and rehearsed and met and communicated clearly and followed up on your commitments. Now it's time to ask your prospect one simple question—turn the page to find out how simple it can be. I'll see you in a bit.

—Mike

 **Secret 24** | **The Close**

There are many well-known closing methods in the sales business. You've probably heard of some of these:

- The Red Herring Close
- The Secondary Question Close
- The Sharp Angle Close
- The Lost Sale Close
- The Affirmative No Close
- The Similar Situation Close
- The Buying Criteria Close
- The Assumptive Close
- The Ben Franklin Close
- The Value Added Close
- The Instant Reverse Close
- The Change-Places Close

If you've followed the steps we've explained so far, you shouldn't have to resort to such elaborate closers. Closing should be a seamless process—simple and direct, as in the following example:

Sales Rep: I'd like to go ahead and book this order. Does that work for you?

In the course of our research, we submitted these closing questions to our buyers and asked for their comments:

A. We can arrange delivery for the 15th, no problem. Is there anything else you need to know to move ahead with this order?

B. If we can arrange delivery on the 15th, can you think of any reason why we shouldn't set it up now?

C. Let's arrange for delivery on the 15th, is that okay?

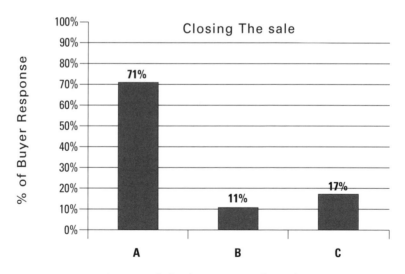

71 % of the buyers preferred question A (provided by Art Sobczak, President of Business by Phone Inc.— see page 54 for more of his contributions).

The Buyers Comment

Jason Wihnon, *Supply Purchaser*	"Question A is an eight out of ten. It tells the customer that the rep has everything in place for the sale to go through providing nothing else is required. It's direct but not overly pushy."
Roy Sekigawa, *Purchasing Operations Manager, Foremost Dairies Hawaii*	"Question A gets an eight out of ten. It shows that the seller actually wants the best for the buyer by asking if additional info is required to meet the buyer's complete satisfaction."
Robert Romero, CPIM, *Supply Chain Manager, Superior Communications*	"Question A deserves seven out of ten. It is more considerate, sincere, and makes it seem as though you really are interested in taking care of the customer."
Kathi Wilson, *Facilities Assistant, IDX Systems Corporation*	"Question A rates ten out of ten. It illustrates that you can provide the service on the terms the buyer needs, and the open-ended question allows communication. It's informal, flows well and it's not pushy."
Anonymous	"I like Question A and rate it an eight out of ten because it's asking me if we need anything further, and they've already said they can make arrangements to deliver when I need it."
Lisa Perdue, *Senior Buyer*	"Question A is nine out of ten. It sounds more professional, more customer-service-oriented. Question B, 'Can you think of any reason why we shouldn't set it up now?' sounds a little pushy."
Anonymous	"Question A gets ten out of ten. I don't like the pressure of the other two. A is direct, it is specific, and he's asking if there's anything else he can do for us."

The Buyers Comment *cont'd*

Lupe Rodriguez, *Facilities Coordinator*	"Question A is my favorite and I rate it seven out of ten. Asking if there's anything else you need to know is a good idea. The more information that's confirmed at the end of a conversation the better; that way nothing is forgotten and there are no mistakes."
Phyllis Pierce, *Purchasing/Accounts Receivable Manager*	"I give Question A ten out of ten. It is more subtle than the other two questions. I like the fact that it asks the buyer if there is anything more that the selling company can do."

MAINTAINING

The good news is that it takes less time to retain a customer than to create a new one. But it's tremendously important to stay in tune with your existing customers' needs. It can lead to quality referrals, and the rapid broadening of your network as one referral leads to another.

Business people can do their colleagues a valuable favor by referring good sales reps. However, it hurts a buyer's reputation when a rep they refer turns out to be incompetent, or not focused on their colleagues' needs. When you deal excellently with your buyers, you boost their confidence in referring you.

The goal of this section is to keep you aware of your existing customers' needs, and to help you appreciate the lifetime value of each of your customers.

Talk to you in Section 7.

—Mike

"With most sales reps, there is not enough follow-up after the sale. Service after the sale is just as important as service before the sale. Buyers want to know that the people they are dealing with, and investing their money and time in, are going to be around for the long term."

— TRENT N. BAKER, C.P.M., Purchasing Manager,
Wilson Foods, Division of Reser's Fine Foods, Inc.

 **Secret 25** **Customer-Satisfaction Email**

It takes a lot of time and effort to acquire a customer, so it makes sense to be proactive about ensuring their complete satisfaction. If you ask, a customer may tell you there's a problem—but if you don't, they may just take their business elsewhere. By sending a brief email at appropriate intervals, you let your customer know they are valued, and you may get the chance to nip any problems in the bud.

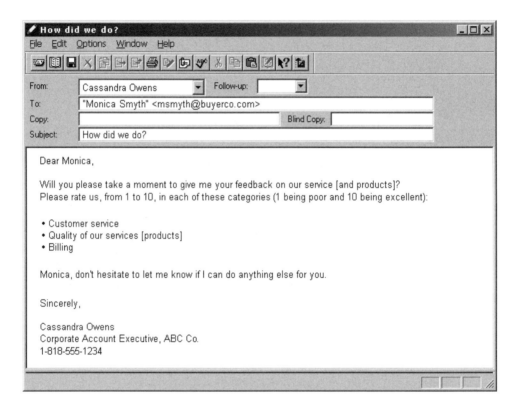

Example: Follow-up message

(Use "services" and/or "products" appropriately)

We asked the Buyers: What percentage of sales reps contact you after the sale to make sure everything went well, and to ensure your ongoing satisfaction?

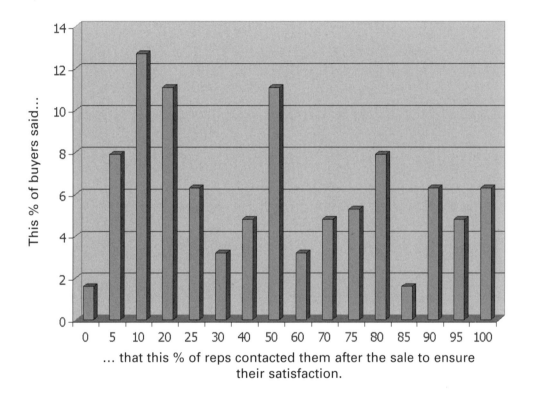

... that this % of reps contacted them after the sale to ensure their satisfaction.

Summary: The majority of buyers said that **more than half of the reps did not follow up** after sales.

We asked the Buyers: On a scale of 1 to 10 (10 being highest), how important is post-sale follow-up?

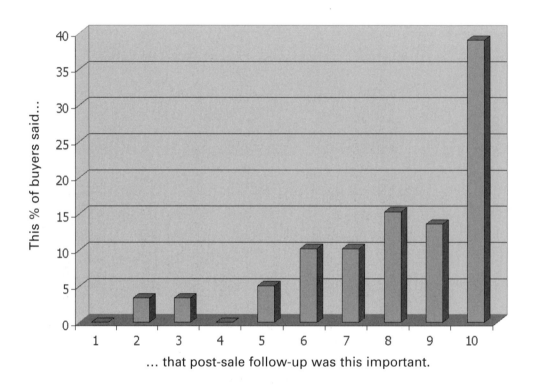

... that post-sale follow-up was this important.

Summary: Over 75% of the buyers felt that post-sale follow-up was **highly important**.

The Buyers Comment

Charles Tobler, **C.P.M., MPP,** *Senior Buyer*	"Many times a salesperson has made an impression on me and I've bought from him. But the next time I needed the product, I couldn't remember the names of the rep or company. Why? Because I never heard from them again after the sale. You must [maintain your] name and product recognition with the buyer."
Thea Bremer, *Buyer*	"This type of survey would tell me that they are truly interested in doing business with me and providing me with the best service that they can."
Cathy Cooper, *Vice President,* *Marketing Manager,* *Washington Federal Savings*	"Another post-sale problem is when companies have turnover among their reps and the company doesn't bother to assign somebody for continued follow-up. I dislike having to track down a sales manager to figure out how to buy from their company again. New reps should demand prior sales records so they can follow up with the clients of the reps they replace."

"I value service and communication above all else. It would be helpful if sales reps could present new and innovative ideas and share any relevant information."

— *HILLARY BERK, Group Manager of Marketing, Supply Chain, Elizabeth Arden*

 **Secret 26**   **Information and Resources**

It's important to follow up with customers, but buyers are busy people; they simply don't have time for phone calls and visits without a specific purpose. So how does a sales professional maintain contact with customers without being annoying?

One way is to give your customers useful information and resources. This is a good way to build strong business relationships and customer loyalty.

Examples:

■ Forward your customers noteworthy articles or information relevant to their industry.

■ Provide your customers with referrals.

■ Conduct objective information-based seminars (see page 24).

The Buyers Comment

Kristen Mitchell, *Senior Buyer, Boston Financial Data Services Incorporated*	"My office-supply vendor once brought together different manufacturers that they deal with and hosted a session [about] products that were of potential value to us."
Bruce R. Weener, *Vice President Customer Satisfaction, American Seating Company*	"Training definitely adds value to the relationship after the sale in terms of technology, new materials, and new processes. I like to be kept informed. Communicate, communicate, communicate."
Wm. Frank Quiett, **C.P.M., A.P.P.,** *Project Lead, Supply Chain Management and Strategic Sourcing*	"The most effective thing a sales rep can do for me after the sale is to follow-up with confirmation on activities associated with the sale, *without being asked!* If I have to ask, that is not customer satisfaction—that is customer problem resolution. If the action comes before the customer has to ask, that is proactive team building and the beginning of a collaborative relationship."
Greg Tennyson, **C.P.M., CPCM,** *Vice President, Corporate Procurement, Oracle Corporation*	"[The supplier] could step back and look at relevant business processes to see how we can re-engineer them together to be more efficient and effective. The supplier could [then] meet with us to explore areas where they might be able to provide some cost savings."
Richard K. Tyler, **C.P.M.,** *Director of Purchasing, MRC Bearings*	"I consider sales reps the experts in their respective areas. As such, I expect them to come to me continually with ways to reduce cost and improve value."

COMMUNICATING

High-level business communicators live in a world of clarity. They can't stand the "gray zone". They know that effective communication is the thread that ties the sales process together, and that it keeps relationships alive once the sale is made.

Communication mastery—few things are more important, if you want to maximize your sales and your business and life potentials. The goal of this section is to help you be that communication master.

Enjoy this section. I'll see you in a while.

—Mike

"Follow-up is tremendously important and an email would be fine. I'll give you an example of what happens more often than not: I'll ask for a usage history or some other documentation, and they'll pass it on to their administrative staff. Then they walk in the next month and say, 'So what can we do for you?' I'll say, 'I'm still waiting for that usage report from last month,' and he'll say, 'What do you mean? I told my office to take care of that.' Why didn't he take ownership and follow up for me with his own company?"

— *KENNETH F. ESBIN, Purchasing Manager, Tarmac America*

 **Secret 27** **Accountability**

Buyer's side of the desk: Buyers tell us that too many sales reps overpromise and underdeliver. How would you feel if you were a buyer and you had to chase a rep down to follow through on a commitment? Would that inspire confidence?

Dependability is a valued commodity in business—yet it's not uncommon for busy sales reps to make promises they don't keep. The problem is time. There is never enough—and an unscheduled item on a to-do list routinely gets bumped by items that do have target dates. By committing to a target date, promises become practical, and you become accountable.

Depending on the situation, the next step would be to confirm completion of the task/promise/commitment via email or with a short voicemail message.

We asked the Buyers: On a scale of 1 to 10 (10 being highest), how useful is it when a rep makes a brief follow-up call or emails you to confirm the fulfillment of a promise?

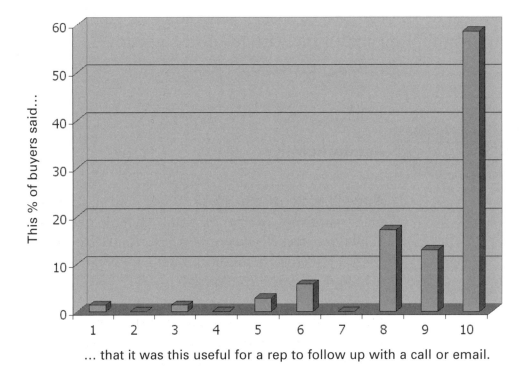

... that it was this useful for a rep to follow up with a call or email.

Summary: Almost 90% of the buyers felt it was **very useful** when reps confirmed they had fulfilled their promises.

We asked the Buyers: What percentage of reps consistently confirm the fulfillment of their promises?

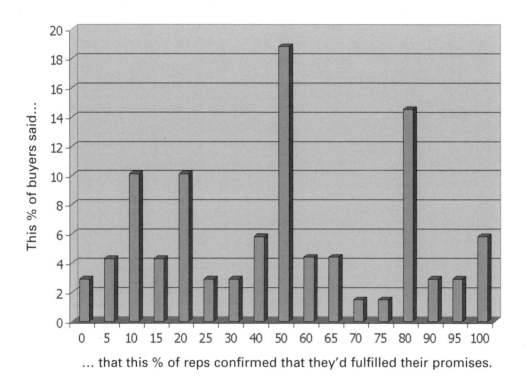

... that this % of reps confirmed that they'd fulfilled their promises.

Summary: The majority of buyers said that **only half** of the reps confirmed that they'd fulfilled their promises.

The Buyers Comment

Greg Graham, *Buyer,* *Kenworth Truck Company*	"I like this approach because it suggests they are competent professionals who follow through, and that raises my comfort level."
David Frieder, *Purchasing Director, Planet* *Automotive Group Inc.*	"[Only] about 20% of the reps I've dealt with are true pros [who] always follow up to ensure the whole job is done—and done right."
Anonymous	"If a sales rep cannot keep a commitment, I would rather hear the truth [instead of] excuses. As a buyer, I have to communicate the status of various components to our entire internal group (manufacturing, production, etc). If you rely on a commitment made by the seller, and the commitment turns out to be false, the buyer is the one who takes all the blame."
Alan B. Rifkin, *Senior Buyer*	"I would like to hear from reps so that I can pass the information on to the appropriate people in my company who would want to be in the loop to know the promised transaction has been completed. It helps keep me on top of things. I deal with several reps who don't always follow through on promises and I find that extremely annoying."
Andrew Jules DeGiulio, *Purchasing Manager*	"Accountability is essential to the business transaction. It flows both ways as does respect. A salesperson who sets a realistic target date and confirms completion earns my respect and therefore the privilege to expand the business relationship."

"I won't return messages that are not decipherable, use poor grammar, or make no real point. You have only one opportunity to get it right, so rehearse the call, and make sure that what you say has substance. Once you leave the message, you can't take it back."

— *ERROL VAN EDEMA, Manager of Purchasing & Manufacturing/Distribution*

 **Secret 28** **Voicemail**

Considering the importance of voicemail, there is a real lack of guidance in the art of effective messages.

How often have you had to play a voicemail message several times because you could not understand the caller's name or phone number? And how many rambling and unplanned messages have you had to endure? How can you avoid this pitfall with your own voicemail messages?

Here are some key steps to ensure clarity and professionalism:

1. ***Plan and prepare.*** Before you make the call, assume the prospect will be busy and that you will have to leave a message. Script out the essential points of your message.

2. ***Rehearse or role-play.*** A quick run run-through helps ensure your message will be communicated clearly and concisely.

3. ***Start and end the message with your number.*** Begin *and* end your message by *clearly* stating your name, company name, and phone number.

We asked the Buyers: What percentage of reps' voicemail messages are difficult to understand, missing key information, or must be played several times to identify the name or phone number?

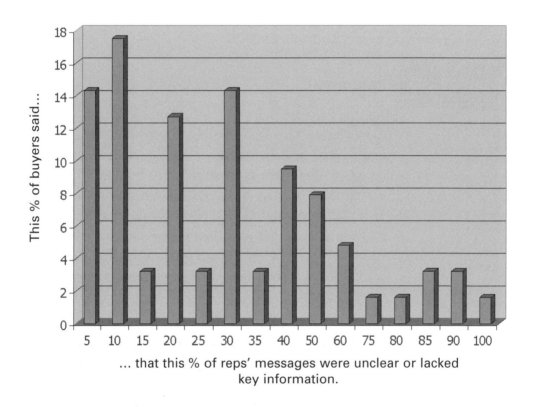

... that this % of reps' messages were unclear or lacked key information.

Summary: The majority of buyers said that over 75% of reps' voicemail was **unclear and lacked key information**.

We asked the Buyers: On a scale of 1 to 10 (10 being highest), how important are effective voicemail messages to you?

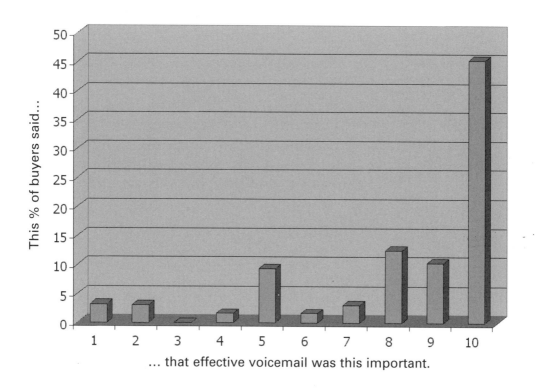

... that effective voicemail was this important.

Summary: The majority of buyers said that effective voicemail was **very important**.

The Buyers Comment

Beckie Beard, **C.P.M, A.P.P, CACM,** *Director, Purchasing &* *Materials Management,* *Lansing Community College*	"Many sales reps do not rehearse what they are going to say, or they speak way too fast. Keep messages short and sweet, and only leave a telephone number if (1) it is a local telephone call; or (2) it is an 800 number. Don't ask customers to return your call long-distance!"
Lou Riley, *Senior Director,* *Materials Management*	"I think that messages should be clear and to the point. I receive many calls throughout the day, and I don't have time to listen to someone go on and on."
Judy Elrite, **C.P.M.,** *Buyer Specialist*	"Most reps say the phone number so fast that it takes three 'listens' to get it. If the message is poorly delivered, I won't return the call. My job is phone-intensive and I'm very busy."

 **Secret 29** **Role-Plays**

Recording role-plays with a colleague can help improve your ability to communicate effectively and intelligently. By taping yourself, you may discover communication habits you were unaware of and could improve upon. During our research, we found that very few reps do this, yet those who did reported dramatic improvements in their confidence and communication skills. As a result, they made more appointments and closed more sales.

Clearly, it's important to make a positive impression when speaking with prospects and customers. When listening to your tape, check for the following signs:

- Are you speaking too quickly?

- Do you sound unsure of yourself?

- Do you speak in a monotone?

- Do you sound insincere?

- Are you talking over the other person?

- Are you using inflection to convey energy and impact where required?

 **Secret 30** | **Weak Words**

Using your taped role-plays (Secret 29), identify and work on eliminating weak, indecisive phrases and words such as

- "Do you know what I mean?"
- "To tell you the truth …"
- "To be honest with you …"
- "I guess"
- "I hope"
- "I think"
- "Maybe"
- "Sort of"
- "Kind of"
- "Probably"
- "Possibly"
- "Basically"
- "Hopefully"

Planning Guide: Write down some of the weak words you tend to use and would like to remove from your business vocabulary.

"Having a backup contact is very helpful, I would rate this 8 out of 10. It saves time, and keeps communication between our companies open and accessible."

— *BRIAN MORAN, Director, Americas' Supply Management, Siemens Westinghouse Power Corporation*

 **Secret 31** **Backup**

Buyer's side of the desk: When a customer needs a quick answer and you're not available, should they have to wait while your staff looks for information only you have access to? No. Make it a priority to introduce all of your clients to someone at your company who can cover for you when you can't be there.

You can introduce your backup with a three-way call, or simply give the buyer your backup's business card. Be sure your backup can access and fully understand all of your relevant account information, so that they can fill in for you effectively.

The Buyers Comment

Leslie Champion,
*Senior Procurement
Specialist, Industrial Design
& Construction, Inc.*

"I find it quite helpful to have a backup contact when I need information. Nothing is more annoying than not being able to get answers when you need them."

Anthony Natali,
C.P.M., A.P.P.,
*National Purchasing
Manager*

"The lack of a knowledgeable backup contact is extremely irritating. A person who answers the phone in the Customer Service department should not be considered a backup."

Lori Patten,
*Director of
Projects–Development,
Hyatt Hotels Corporation*

"Most reps don't provide a regular backup contact, but it would definitely be helpful. It's frustrating having to spend so much time sifting through company voicemail directories trying to find someone to answer my question (when my sales rep is not available)."

Tina M. Lowenthal,
*Associate Director of
Purchasing Services,
California Institute
of Technology*

"Providing a backup person is an effective way for sales reps to provide better service. One of our large suppliers always has backup contacts in place and since we work closely together, it makes for a great working relationship.It's much easier to work with them."

"An email summary would be very helpful; it's always good to have written clarification of key points. It shows they're paying attention and that they're on top of things. In five years, perhaps 2% of the reps I've met with have ever emailed a written summary of key points after a meeting."

— *KRISTEN MITCHELL, Senior Buyer, Boston Financial Data Services Incorporated*

 **Secret 32** **Written Key Point Summary**

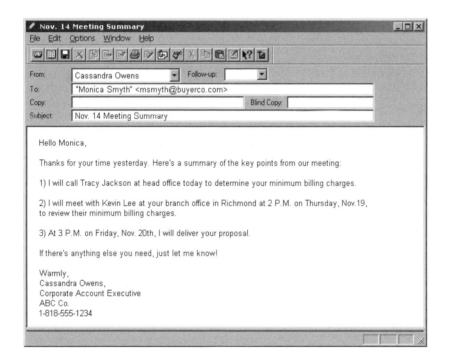

Email summaries of key points discussed is a great way to ensure effective communication and accountability, and provides an opportunity for the other party to add any points of their own.

The Buyers Comment

Jeffrey J. Dodig,
ForestCity Residential,
National Accounts Manager

"I think emailing a summary after the first meeting is important, because I don't want to do business with the guy that's just trying to make a quick sale or isn't interested in doing follow-up—and I never hear from him again."

Dean R. Schlosser, jr.,
Purchasing Agent

"An email summary would be very helpful. I always take notes at meetings and it would be helpful to compare the rep's summary with mine."

Chris Nield,
Corporate Buyer,
International Truck
and Engine Corp.

"It's very important, especially for buyers that don't have meeting minutes. I usually have meeting minutes, which I usually send to all involved. So an email summary and minutes for comparison would be very helpful."

Hillary Berk,
Group Manager of
Marketing, Supply Chain,
Elizabeth Arden

"It's called follow-up and after working twelve hours it's helpful to have a reminder!"

Ken Fuqua,
Purchasing Administrator

"I find this very useful since it allows me to start an email file to keep track of my relationship with the vendor."

Krysia Diaz, CEBS,
Benefits Supervisor

"That would be great—very helpful, because many times we put stuff aside when we are busy with all the things going on in our department. There is always something that we need to focus our attention on, so when we get the email it's just nice to have that to refer back to when necessary."

The Buyers Comment *cont'd*

Randy Shepherd,
Systems Coordinator,
Senior Buyer

"I always ask for a follow-up email from the rep after the meeting to help me communicate with my colleagues and keep everything organized and filed."

We asked the Buyers: On a scale of 1 to 10 (10 being highest),
how helpful is it when a rep emails you a
summary of your meeting's key points?

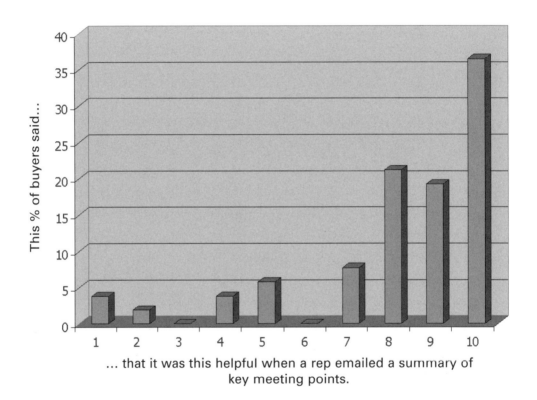

... that it was this helpful when a rep emailed a summary of
key meeting points.

Summary: Over 75% of the buyers said an email summary
was **extremely helpful**.

We asked the Buyers: What percentage of reps email you summaries of your meetings' key points?

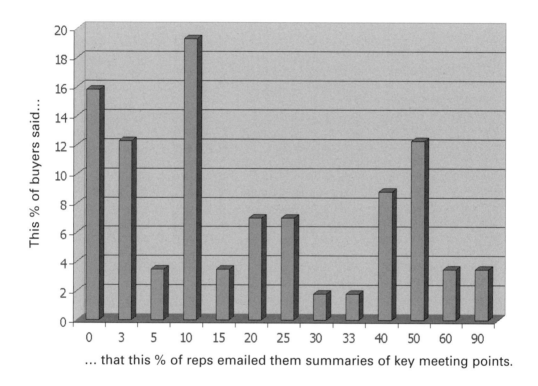

... that this % of reps emailed them summaries of key meeting points.

Summary: The majority of buyers said that **fewer than 25%** of reps sent email summaries.

ANNOYING

We've covered a lot of ground, dealing with proactive approaches that add value to your buyer relationships. However, this book would not be complete without this next section with its tongue-in-cheek title.

Have you ever had a situation where you did everything right, until you did one devastatingly wrong thing? Or perhaps a sale seemed to be going smoothly, then suddenly "tanked" for no apparent reason? If so, you may realize that knowing what not to do is as important as knowing what to do.

The goal of this section is to acquaint you with common sales mistakes, so you can avoid them. I hope you enjoy the read. I'll be back one last time at the end of the book. See you then!

—Mike

Secret 33 — How to Annoy Buyers—Guaranteed

When it comes to creating and keeping customers, it's also important to know what not to do.

We asked the buyers to tell us about annoying things sales reps sometimes do. We have placed their responses into the following categories:

- Being unprepared for meetings

- Overpromising and underdelivering

- Back-door selling

- Being insincere or concealing information

- Continuously cold-calling or showing up without an appointment

- Being too persistent or aggressive

- Talking too much; showing poor listening skills

- Failing to do post-sale follow-up

The Buyers Comment

Being unprepared for meetings

Anne Stilwell
Director, Contract and Procurement Services, Fannie Mae

"I'm not impressed when reps meet with me without doing research on our company. Instead, they use up half of the meeting time asking me for basic information. If they were true professionals, they would have done this before they came to see me. It's also annoying when they fail to plan the meeting so that the important content is covered in the time allocated."

"It is irritating when reps show up at follow-up meetings without having answers to questions that were asked at the initial meeting."

Michael Tator,
V.P., Director of Production, Wunderman, of the Y & R Companies, Irvine

"Being unprepared with their information or material."

"Showing up late for meetings."

"Not telling me that they are bringing additional people to the meeting beforehand."

"Not having the proper equipment for making the presentation."

"Dragging the meeting out too long."

**Judy Elrite,
C.P.M.,**
Buyer Specialist

"It's annoying when reps haven't done their research on my company. I also don't like it when they ask me who the 'other' supplier is. They should know who the competition is in my area."

**Greg Tennyson,
C.P.M., CPCM,**
Vice President, Corporate Procurement, Oracle Corporation

"Coming in and giving a cold pitch and not having done their homework is probably the most annoying thing, because it's a waste of my time, and it's a waste of theirs."

Christopher Locke,
Global Lead Buyer,
DaimlerChrysler Corporation

"It's frustrating when sales reps do not understand our specifications and requirements. They assume they know how we want our equipment built based on prior programs and do not even read the current specs. Another source of frustration is [that the] quote packages they send us clearly show their inability to comprehend what we're asking for. Even the simplest of requests are wrong. For example, I usually ask for three quote packages: two un-priced and one priced. You can't believe the variations I get: two priced and one un-priced; three priced, three un-priced; one un-priced and one priced ..."

Lawrence K. Buker,
C.P.M., CPIM,
Corporate Purchasing/Travel
Manager, QAD Inc.

"It's annoying when I get a call and the rep asks, 'What does your company do?' The first thing I think is: This guy hasn't even gone to our website, or he doesn't even know who he's calling, and I'm not going to take the time to explain ... Reps should already know that before they knock on the door."

Overpromising and underdelivering

Karen Gyarfas-Lavallee,
Studio Manager—Director
of Print Production, Landor
Associates, of the Y & R
Companies, Irvine

"I get annoyed by things like sloppy follow-up, being late for appointments, and not respecting my time."

Anonymous

"Promising things that they are not able to do and price changes without notification are both very annoying."

Vivian Green,
Production Manager,
Wunderman, of the Y & R
Companies, Irvine

"I find it annoying when reps are forgetful (usually because they didn't take notes) or are slow to follow through on delivering information I've requested."

J. Wihnon, *Supply Purchaser*	"It's annoying when they break procedures that are already in place just to close the sale, and then they end up not delivering on the promise. Just be up-front [and] promise what you can deliver. Missing deadlines is terrible. Don't say you can do something knowing you won't be able to."

Back-door Selling

Chuck Stanasek, **C.P.M.,** *Materials Manager*	"An annoying thing is 'back-door selling'—bypassing the procurement group, and dealing directly with the various departments, such as Engineering."
Fred Wilson, *Procurement Manager—* *Industrial Engineer*	"I know one thing that really ticks off buyers: going over their head or around through the back-door. That just doesn't sit very well with me. From that moment on, I'm open to the idea of someone replacing him."
Toni Horn, C.P.M., *Global Commodity Manager,* *Silicon Graphics Inc.*	"It annoys me when reps attempt to rework their way into the company and pitch their products and services to others outside the purchasing department, after we've told them 'No.'"
Kathi Wilson, *Facilities Assistant,* *IDX Systems Corporation*	"I find it frustrating when I have rejected their proposal, and they call back at another time attempting to speak to another buyer! It's unethical and sneaky, and it makes for bad business."
Lawrence K. Buker, **C.P.M., CPIM,** *Corporate Purchasing/Travel* *Manager, QAD Inc.*	"It's annoying when they follow up and I say, 'We're going to have to get back to you,' or 'There's been a delay,' and they start talking to other people in the company to try and advance the sale. This can annoy a buyer so much that the next time an opportunity comes, we don't call them."

Being insincere or concealing information

Linda J. Mahran, *Manager, Non-Product Purchasing, NA*	"One serious annoyance is when the seller calls and doesn't identify what product or service they are offering. Not being up-front is not the way to handle a sales call."
Robert Romero, CPIM, *Supply Chain Manager, Superior Communications*	"Some of the things that annoy me are the sales reps who come across a little too sweet, a little too nice, to the point where you see it's not sincere; it's just a little too sugar-coated. I prefer someone who is more down to earth, truthful and genuine."

Continuously cold-calling or showing up without an appointment

Lisa Perdue, *Senior Buyer*	"Some reps just keep calling and calling. If I don't call back, it's because I don't need their service, or I'm not interested. Constantly calling me and annoying me is going to push me off even farther."
Sharon Spear, *Production Manager, Wunderman, of the Y & R Companies, Irvine*	"I find it very annoying when reps drop by without an appointment."
Stan Marshall, C.P.M., *Purchasing Manager*	"It bothers me when they visit with no appointment. I hate it when they just show up. This will never land them a sale with me."
Sheryl Haeberle, *Buyer, Brigham Young University—Idaho*	"I dislike it when reps just show up without letting me know they are coming. My time is valuable. I often stop buying from repeat offenders."

Christopher Locke, *Global Lead Buyer, DaimlerChrysler Corporation*	"Suppliers who show up unannounced at the buyer's desk and expect a major dialog really frustrate me. For every telephone call, email, and meeting one supplier sets up with the buyer, there are at least a dozen more suppliers calling, emailing, and expecting time for discussion."

Being too persistent or aggressive

Charles B. Detrick, C.P.M, *Purchasing Manager, Harris Automation*	"Overcalling. Reps are always calling, even when I've left a message to tell them that I will get back to them. Sometimes I need to put the rep off because I have to wait for people to get back to me first, so I don't have an answer for a rep at that time, but some keep calling anyway."
James L. Semala, *Buyer/Planner, NISource*	"It's annoying when you get an overabundance of follow-up calls from reps to find out if the successful bidder has been chosen. When you have fifteen people calling you fifteen times each to ask when the decision will be made, it gets frustrating."
Lorna Good, *Senior Production Manager, Wunderman, of the Y & R Companies, Irvine*	"Calling too often! Some reps call to inquire about the status of projects every single day, even after they have been told that they will be contacted if they are awarded the job. I have told these same reps that I am extremely busy and do not have time to call them back, or even listen to unnecessary voicemails, but they keep calling."
Linda J. Mahran, Manager, *Non-Product Purchasing, NA*	"Continuing to sell after I have said that I am not interested is not the way to do business. A little persistence is okay, but going overboard is not."

Cliffton Durham,
Product Manager

"Being far too persistent when I'm not interested. In the future, [even] if this rep has an item that we might need, I would not be inclined to do business with them."

Talking too much; showing poor listening skills

Richard K. Tyler, C.P.M.,
Director of Purchasing,
MRC Bearings

"It's annoying when reps don't listen! Some reps push, push, push, and just want to close the sale. You can't shove yourself down someone's throat."

Trent N. Baker, C.P.M.,
Purchasing Manager,
Wilson Foods, Division of
Reser's Fine Foods, Inc.

"I get annoyed when reps spend most of the time talking about themselves or their company without listening to me and trying to understand my needs and about my company."

David Mizer,
Vice President
Strategic Sourcing,
Carnival Cruise Lines Inc.

"The biggest thing that annoys me about reps is that they don't listen. You can have a meeting with a rep and explain what your parameters are in business, what your limitations are, what your decision process is and why, maybe at that time, their service is not something that you can pursue. But some of them don't hear you. They continue to push and push, and that's very irritating. The problem is that it really puts that sales rep in a negative position for any and all future contact for business, because you don't want to have to deal with an aggressive salesperson."

Roy Sekigawa,
Purchasing Operations
Manager,
Foremost Dairies Hawaii

"It's annoying when reps assume what the buyer's needs are before asking. Too much talk, not enough questions."

Failing to do post-sale follow-up

Anonymous	"Servicing the sale, after the contract is signed, is often ignored—yet that's when service has to be at its best, to keep the new customer."
Jeffrey J. Dodig, *ForestCity Residential, National Accounts Manager*	"I dislike reps who make the sale—and then that's it. When you have questions or you need help, or your users need to be trained, all of a sudden they're very difficult to get hold of … When I need to buy some products, they're there to sell them. When I need some follow-up work, or responses, or help with issues that aren't related to sales, I want to know they're going to be there."
David Frieder, *Purchasing Director, Planet Automotive Group Inc.*	"It's annoying when [reps] make promises they cannot keep to get the account. Too often the rep gets the initial order, and then they forget about us."

Some final thoughts from the author

Here **we are** at the end of the book! I hope you found some specific approaches that made sense for you—approaches which, when used consistently, can become your hallmarks. Sales is not rocket science—it's mostly just common sense. I've tried to make that point with clarity. If you want to make good impressions in your business dealings, it's all about quality communication, building trust, and not wasting the decision-maker's time.

I'm often asked, "Do you use these tips yourself? Do you walk your talk?"

Absolutely! At Approved Publications and Training, it's our official policy to use these tips. I believe that leadership is best done "top down," and that if I expect my staff to follow the principles of ***Buyer-Approved Selling***, that I must do so as well. I'm pleased to report that we get a lot of positive feedback when we send email summaries and Advance Meeting Agendas, and when we use the other tips I have recommended here.

How many reps who read this book actually use the tips?

Given a choice, most people follow the path of least resistance. These tips require extra work—so, regrettably, many reps who read about them won't use them. But what if your company decided a few of the tips in this book should be used each and every time a sales rep interacted with a buyer? What if your company made certain tips policy, and required sales reps to use them "or else"?

Would that be fair? Let's examine it from both sides of the coin.

The buyer's perspective says, "Yes, it's fair! It's about *quid pro quo*, an equal exchange. I give you my business; I deserve to be treated competently and professionally."

The salesperson's perspective *could* say, "It's win-win really. If my company makes a particular Buyer-Approved approach a policy, it will become habit for me—and the buyers I deal with will win. And since this new habit will allow me to differentiate myself from the competition, I'll win more business and earn more commissions."

So how can you lose?

You can't.

If you'd like to get a better sense of how these Buyer-Approved approaches can be used, I've written a book called *The Sales Star*. It follows a first-time sales rep through his first twelve months on the job—at the end of which he wins his company's Sales Rep of the Year award. The book is a story, but it is based on the real world of sales. It brings the tips in this book to life, and shows you how you can expect your buyers to react to them.

The following page includes Mitch Bardwell's foreword to *The Sales Star*. Mitch is the Director & Assistant General Manager of the Sales Training Division for Canon U.S.A. He makes some key points I think you will appreciate, as you pursue your goal of becoming the best sales professional *you* can be—one of the Top 20 Percenters.

Sincerely,

MIKE SCHELL
mschell@approvedseries.com

From *The Sales Star:*
Foreword by Mitch Bardwell

In Canon's Sales Training division we have a maxim, "knowledge shared, momentum gained." It speaks to one of our core principles of communicating *ideas that work* among our sales channels. After all, spreading the knowledge of applications and techniques that tip the scales in your favor is one of the hallmarks of a great sales organization.

It was with this thought in mind that I distributed complimentary copies of *Buyer-Approved Selling: Sales Strategies from the Buyer's Side of the Desk* to the entire Canon sales force last year. Finally, a common-sense look into the psyche of the buyer. Filled with lessons based on real-world experiences, it provided a solid framework for sales rep behavior, strategies and tips for improving success.

The Sales Star takes it to the next level. It's about *applying* the techniques discussed in *Buyer-Approved Selling*. It's about embracing the idea that there's no getting around serious, hard work if you want to come out on top. But just reading a book to enhance sales performance doesn't guarantee results—you've got to *live* it.

This book cuts right to the chase and takes you on a step-by-step journey through the eyes of Jack, a new sales representative who wants to be the best, but doesn't quite know how to go about it. I think this book is a great opportunity for any salesperson to step into Jack's shoes and gain another perspective on the art of selling… anything.

This book says, "work hard *NOW*," "set your goals *NOW*," "put the systems and behaviors in place *NOW*," to achieve even greater success later. And it does so by presenting viable examples of the common sense advice delivered in *Buyer-Approved Selling*. What to say, when to say it, and how to say it. This book demystifies what it takes to be a top salesperson.

It's one thing to learn something; it is another to apply it. This book will help you do both.

—Mitch Bardwell, Director & Assistant General Manager
Sales Training Division
Canon U.S.A., Inc.

Buyer Contributions

Grahame Gill	Facilities Buyer 8, 44, 56
Lorna Good	Senior Production Manager Wunderman, of the Y&R Companies, Irvine 146
Greg Graham	Buyer Kenworth Truck Company 75, 124
Vivian Green	Production Manager Wunderman, of the Y&R Companies, Irvine 143
Karen Gyarfas-Lavallee	Studio Manager-Director of Print Production Landor Associates, of the Y&R Companies, Irvine 143
Sheryl Haeberle	Buyer Brigham Young University, Idaho 41, 85, 145
Jim Haining **C.P.M., A.P.P., MBA**	Manager, Corporate Agreements 41, 80
Jeff Hardman	Director of Network Operations 44
Joe Hoffman	Commodity Manager III 85
Toni Horn **C.P.M.**	Global Commodity Manager Silicon Graphics Inc. 63, 80, 144
Gregory W. Hunter	Manager of Purchasing Cannon USA 45
Wendy Imamura, **C.P.M., CPPB, CMIR**	Material Processing Center Manager Verizon Hawaii Inc. 23, 28, 59, 85
Peggy Jones	Operations/H.R. Director Magic Software Enterprises, Inc. 89, 101

INDEX

Charts

The Author/CEO of Approved Publications and Training

A respected teacher of sales and marketing skills with more than 20 years of corporate sales experience, **Michael Schell** is the Author/CEO of Approved Publications and Training. The companies produce, market, and license the Approved Series of books and associated workshops.

Mike's 20-year background in business-to-business sales includes ten years in highly-competitive, commissioned-based fields, where he had many opportunities to learn things the hard way.

When Mike is not writing books, speaking, training, or working with his talented staff, he can be found playing guitar on a beach or jamming with the boys in his "basement" rock band. He enjoys spending time cycling, making his friends laugh, traveling, and jumping out of airplanes.

The Publisher/CEO of the Marketshare Research Institute

Mitch Merker, Publisher and CEO of the Marketshare Research Institute is an accomplished business professional with over 18 years of front-line experience focusing on telephone-based marketing/research campaigns.

Mitch spent 16 years building a career in the industrial electronics industry, gaining expertise in business-to-business sales and sales management. As Marketshare expanded its sales and research divisions, Mitch used his knowledge of systems and process management to create predictable, effective experiences for Marketshare's clients and employees.

When Mitch is not conducting research projects, speaking, training, or working on the business at hand, he can be found with his wonderful wife Eva and their loving black lab, Indy, on a nature trail or dog-friendly beach. Mitch also likes cycling, making his friends laugh, good movies, traveling, and beating Mike at Scrabble.

About the Company

How the Approved Series™ began

During his 20 years in corporate sales, author Mike Schell attended many sales seminars and read nearly 100 books on selling. He often wondered

■ Why did sales authors and speakers take so much time to explain simple concepts, and to describe specific, practical ways to use them?

■ How did the methods they recommended work in the real world?

■ Where was the validation from the people who mattered most—the buyers?

Mike realized that the book he was looking for had not been written: a book from the perspective of the people who were sold to. These were people who had met and interacted with countless sales reps; people who knew exactly what worked and what didn't. Who could explain selling better than **professional buyers**?

The result was *Buyer-Approved Selling*—a book filled with practical, no-nonsense tips recommended by buyers themselves.

Buyer-Approved Selling was immediately embraced by the corporate community, and executives have commissioned custom editions of the book for their companies. Mike has been invited to lead special Buyer-Approved training seminars, and is highly in demand as a keynote speaker. He brings dynamic personal style and great energy to his presentations of the Approved experience, conveying a wealth of insight and advice with refreshing directness and inspiring immediacy. Backed by extensive research and his own first-hand knowledge of sales, Mike's approach engages audiences by illustrating and illuminating the Buyer-Approved sales secrets in a concrete, ready-to-use form they can apply to their own careers right away.

How the Approved Series works for you

The **Approved Series** focuses on the opinions of the decision-makers who are most important to you and your work:

Approved Series Reader	Decision-makers	Approved Series title
Sales representative	Professional buyers	*Buyer-Approved Selling*
Small-business owner	Customers	*The Customer-Approved Small Business*
Job seeker	Employers	*Human Resource-Approved Job Interviews & Resumes*

Each **Approved Series** book gives you a complete step-by-step plan for achieving the results you seek, based on real advice from the people you want to influence. In addition to their recommended techniques, you'll find many of their actual comments—as they explain, in their own words, why some actions work and some fail. (The answers may surprise you.)

It's one thing to read a book, and another to apply it. With the **Approved Series**, you can work with confidence—knowing the techniques you use come from "the other side of the desk." It makes all the difference!

THE APPROVED SERIES

Ask us about:

- **Utilizing the Approved Series in corporate promotions**
- **Customized publications**
- **Bulk orders**
- **Customized "Approved Booklets" and "Approved Book Chapters"**
- **Keynote speaking**
- **Training workshops**

For inquiries and orders call toll free 877.870.0009
or visit us online at www.approvedseries.com

Buyer-Approved Selling

A selling guide for salespeople that is based on an extensive expert survey of what today's business buyers want in the process of buying. Based on more than 4,000 carefully-asked questions of business buyers, this best-of-breed selling guide is indisputably an advance in sales science. Any sales professional selling to the modern business world stands to profit considerably from using *Buyer-Approved Selling*.

$19.95 US/$24.95 Canada

The Sales Star

Written as the companion guide to *Buyer-Approved Selling*, *The Sales Star* tells the story of a determined new sales rep named Jack. One of 73 sales reps in a 350 person company, Jack is left to fend for himself. From the foreword by Mitch Bardwell, Director & Assistant General Manager, Sales Training Division, Canon U.S.A., Inc.: "This book takes it to the next level. It's about applying the techniques discussed in *Buyer-Approved Selling*. It's about embracing the idea that there's no getting around serious, hard work if you want to come out on top."

$14.95 US/$19.95 Canada

The Customer-Approved Small Business

An easy-to-read, easy-to-use book that guides a business owner through two critical business areas: Laying a solid foundation (so customers will find dealing with you easy and enjoyable) and business development (creating and retaining customers).

$19.95 US/$24.95 Canada

Human Resource-Approved Job Interviews and Resumes

If you've ever wondered what prospective employers really think of your resume, or if you're concerned about making a good impression in the all-critical job interview, read this book! Easy to read and easy to use, *Human Resource-Approved Job Interviews and Resumes* provides practical tips and strategies to guide you through two critical areas: The resume and the job interview.

$19.95 US/$24.95 Canada